W9-CIP-932

Cross Training

Ultimate Fitness

Fitness, Health & Nutrition was created by Rebus, Inc. and published by Time-Life Books.

REBUS, INC.

Publisher: RODNEY FRIEDMAN
Editorial Director: CHARLES L. MEE JR.

Editor: THOMAS DICKEY
Senior Editor: MARY CROWLEY
Text Editor: LINDA EPSTEIN
Associate Editors: WILLIAM DUNNETT, CARL LOWE
Chief of Research: CARNEY W. MIMMS III
Copy Editor: ROBERT HERNANDEZ
Contributing Editors: JACQUELINE DAMIAN,
JANE SCHECHTER

Art Director: JUDITH HENRY
Associate Art Director: FRANCINE KASS
Designer: SARA BOWMAN
Still Life and Food Photographer: STEVEN MAYS
Exercise Photographer: ANDREW ECCLES
Photo Stylist: LEAH LOCOCO
Contributing Photographer: DAVID MADISON

Test Kitchen Director: GRACE YOUNG
Recipe Editor: BONNIE J. SLOTNICK

Time-Life Books Inc. is a wholly owned subsidiary of

TIME INCORPORATED

Founder: HENRY R. LUCE 1898-1967

Editor-in-Chief: JASON McMANUS
Chairman and Chief Executive Officer: J. RICHARD MUNRO
President and Chief Operating Officer: N.J. NICHOLAS JR.
Corporate Editor: RAY CAVE
Executive Vice President, Books: KELSO F. SUTTON
Vice President, Books: PAUL V. McLAUGHLIN

TIME-LIFE BOOKS INC.

Editor: GEORGE CONSTABLE

Executive Editor: ELLEN PHILLIPS
Director of Design: LOUIS KLEIN
Director of Editorial Resources: PHYLLIS K. WISE
Editorial Board: RUSSELL B. ADAMS JR., DALE M. BROWN,
ROBERTA CONLAN, THOMAS H. FLAHERTY, LEE HASSIG,
DONIA ANN STEELE, ROSALIND STUBENBERG
Director of Photography and Research: JOHN CONRAD
WEISER
Assistant Director of Editorial Resources: ELISE RITTER
GIBSON

President: CHRISTOPHER T. LINEN
Chief Operating Officer: JOHN M. FAHEY JR.
Senior Vice Presidents: ROBERT M. DESENA, JAMES L. MERCER
PAUL R. STEWART
Vice Presidents: STEPHEN L. BAIR, RALPH J. CUOMO,
NEAL GOFF, STEPHEN L. GOLDSTEIN, JUANITA T. JAMES,
HALLETT JOHNSON III, CAROL KAPLAN, SUSAN J.
MARUYAMA, ROBERT H. SMITH, JOSEPH J. WARD
Director of Production Services: ROBERT J. PASSANTINO
Supervisor of Quality Control: JAMES KING

FITNESS, HEALTH & NUTRITION

Cross Training

Ultimate Fitness

Time-Life Books, Alexandria, Virginia

CONSULTANTS FOR THIS BOOK

Paul Asmuth, a world champion marathon swimmer who has competed for more than 20 years, was a three-time All-American in NCAA competition. Since college, Asmuth has won every major swimming marathon at least once and holds the record for five events. He also set a men's world record for swimming the English Channel. In 1982, he was inducted into the International Marathon Swimming Hall of Fame in Fort Lauderdale, Florida.

Richard A. Berger, Ph.D., is professor of exercise physiology at the College of Health, Physical Education, Recreation and Dance at Temple University in Philadelphia. He is the author of *Introduction to Weight Training, Applied Exercise Physiology* and *Physical Conditioning for Men.* Dr. Berger is a member of the American College of Sports Medicine and the American Alliance for Health, Physical Education, Recreation and Dance.

John Howard has been a competitive cyclist and triathlete for the past 20 years. A seven-time United States Cycling Federation champion and a Pan-American Games gold medalist, Howard was a three-time member of the U.S. Olympic cycling team. He also set a world speed record for cycling at 152 mph. Howard conducts bicycling clinics around the United States.

Amy Lyn Kallman, M.A., is the director of public fitness programs at Sports Training Institute in New York City. She is also a private fitness consultant.

Dave Scott is a triathlete whom many consider to be the premier endurance athlete in the world today. He is a six-time winner and undisputed master of the grueling Ironman triathlon, which is held annually in Hawaii, and he has won or placed in numerous other national and international triathlons. A writer and speaker on sports physiology and training, he is the author of *Dave Scott's Triathlon Training Book.*

William Wagner is an exercise specialist at Sports Training Institute.

Nutritional Consultants

Ann Grandjean, Ed.D., is Associate Director of the Swanson Center for Nutrition, Omaha, Neb.; chief nutrition consultant to the U.S. Olympic Committee; and an instructor in the Sports Medicine Program, Orthopedic Surgery Department, University of Nebraska Medical Center.

Myron Winick, M.D., is the R.R. Williams Professor of Nutrition, Professor of Pediatrics, Director of the Institute of Human Nutrition, and Director of the Center for Nutrition, Genetics and Human Development at Columbia University College of Physicians and Surgeons. He has served on the Food and Nutrition Board of the National Academy of Sciences and is the author of many books, including *Your Personalized Health Profile.*

For information about any Time-Life book please call 1-800-621-7026, or write:
Reader Information
Time-Life Customer Service
P.O. Box C-32068
Richmond, Virginia 23261-2068

TIME-LIFE is a trademark of Time Incorporated U.S.A.

Library of Congress Cataloging-in-Publication Data
Cross training: ultimate fitness.
    p. cm. — (Fitness, health & nutrition; vol. 16)
    Includes index.
    ISBN 0-8094-6126-9.
    ISBN 0-8094-6127-7 (lib. bdg.)
    1. Triathlon—Training. I. Time-Life Books. II. Series: Fitness, health, and nutrition; vol. 16.
GV1060.775.T73C76   1989
796.4'07—dc19   88-29510
                                 CIP

This book is not intended as a substitute for the advice of a physician or an athletic coach. Readers who have or suspect they may have specific medical problems should consult a physician before beginning any program of strenuous physical exercise.

CONTENTS

CHAPTER ONE

Total Conditioning

The benefits — and pleasures — of expanding your training program

Many people who take up exercise find themselves choosing and sticking with a single activity or workout. However, a growing number of fitness enthusiasts and athletes are expanding their exercise regimens through cross training — building and maintaining fitness by training in more than one activity. The benefits of cross training range from injury prevention to relief from boredom, and this chapter presents the merits, the challenges and the debates about this relatively new method of rounding out an exercise program. It will also show you how to practice cross training in a manageable schedule. Because many cross trainers begin as runners primarily, the exercise chapters in this book focus largely on cycling and swimming, the two most popular alternatives for building aerobic fitness. And if you want to compete, you can use this overview of cross training as your guide to combine all three activities into a training program for a triathlon — the ultimate test of conditioning for strength, versatility and endurance.

Cross Training:
A Total-Body Regimen

Training in a variety of sports conditions many more muscles than any one sport can. The illustrations show the primary and secondary muscle groups (primary muscles are those that are used directly to perform an activity; secondary muscles assist the primary muscle group) exercised in swimming, cycling and running; in a cross training program, each of these activities complements the others in building overall strength and muscular endurance. Swimming primarily conditions the upper body muscles, which are directly responsible for propulsion. Cycling relies mainly on front of thigh and back muscles, while running emphasizes opposing muscles along the back of the leg.

Primary muscle groups ●
Secondary muscle groups ●

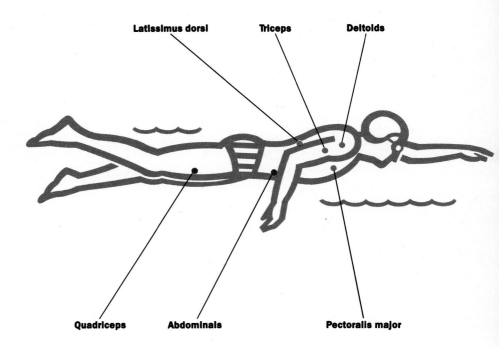

Latissimus dorsi   Triceps   Deltoids

Quadriceps   Abdominals   Pectoralis major

Who uses cross training?

In recent years, many athletes, especially endurance athletes, have claimed that the fitness benefits derived from training in several sports or modes of exercise can result in better overall conditioning as well as improved performance in one or more of the activities. To what extent cross training can increase performance potential is widely debated. Other benefits, as discussed below, are more clear-cut, and certainly cross training has become a popular method of staying fit. Runners are particularly drawn to some form of cross training: In a survey of recreational runners, more than 90 percent reported that they engaged in another sport or endurance activity habitually, with cycling and swimming the leading preferences. And since the late 1970s, cross training — or expanded training, as it is also called — has been popularized as the exercise regimen used by triathletes, who typically train and compete in swimming, cycling and running, and are considered by many experts to be the best-conditioned athletes in the world.

Unless you want to be a triathlete, is cross training really a worthwhile pursuit?

Anyone who is intent on maintaining a program of aerobic exercise can derive benefits from cross training. One compelling reason for

Latissimus dorsi   Erector spinae   Trapezius

External obliques

Gluteus maximus

Quadriceps   Wrist extensors

Trapezius

Gluteus maximus

Hamstrings

Abdominals

Quadriceps

Soleus   Gastrocnemius

runners to cross train is that substituting activities like cycling and swimming for some of their workout runs will diffuse the physical stress of running, thereby reducing the risk of injury. Not only are swimming and cycling low-impact activities compared to running, but each conditions distinctly different muscle groups as well as some of the same muscles in different ways. In endurance workouts, injuries may result when one muscle group becomes stronger than an opposing one. Doing a greater variety of exercise reduces the chance of creating this kind of imbalance and thus the chance of suffering pulled muscles or knee injuries.

If you do sustain an injury from one activity, you can maintain your cardiovascular conditioning while you recover by training in another activity that exercises different muscles. Swimming is excellent for either runners or cyclists who suffer leg injuries, since the driving force of swimming is powered by the muscles of the upper body. In addition, swimming helps develop your upper and lower body more uniformly than running or cycling alone.

Performing two or three different endurance exercises also affords a mental change of pace that can make working out more enjoyable. And if you are starting a new activity, you will usually experience relatively rapid improvement, which is also a great motivator. Finally, whether you cross train to supplement a primary exercise or devote

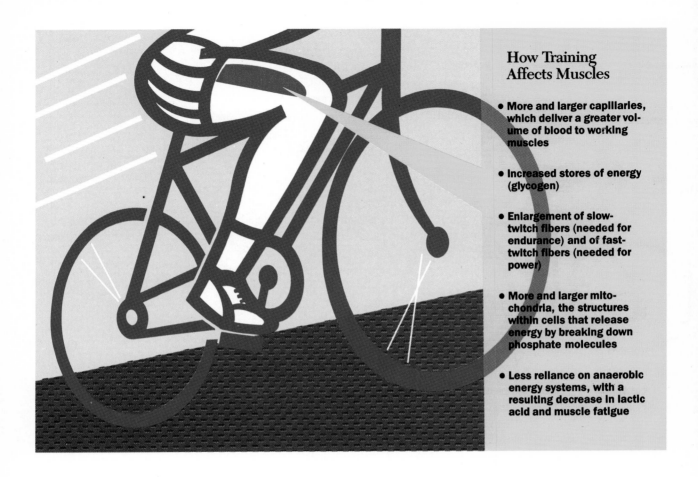

How Training Affects Muscles

- More and larger capillaries, which deliver a greater volume of blood to working muscles

- Increased stores of energy (glycogen)

- Enlargement of slow-twitch fibers (needed for endurance) and of fast-twitch fibers (needed for power)

- More and larger mitochondria, the structures within cells that release energy by breaking down phosphate molecules

- Less reliance on anaerobic energy systems, with a resulting decrease in lactic acid and muscle fatigue

Muscles undergo profound cellular and metabolic changes with training, as outlined in the chart above. The increase in capillaries and the changes in mitochondria allow a muscle to use oxygen more effectively, while the improved retention of glycogen (the stored form of carbohydrate) means more energy for work. Muscle fiber contraction is faster and stronger. Also, the fibers do not tire as easily, in part because of the more efficient processing of lactic acid, a by-product of energy metabolism associated with fatigue.

equal amounts of effort to several activities, you will feel in greater overall shape and have better muscle development than if you perform just a single sport or exercise.

Is it true that training different muscle groups with cross training can better your performance in a particular activity?
Because every exercise targets specific muscles, most experts believe there is no substitute for training in your own sport if you are a serious competitor. If you want to improve your running speed and endurance significantly, it is necessary to devote virtually all of your training time to running; the same applies to cycling, swimming and any other endurance sport. Some athletes believe that comparatively small amounts of cross training can supplement performance in their chosen sport; however, the most common reason single-sport athletes give for cross training is to maintain aerobic fitness while recovering from an injury. Cross training benefits, therefore, are actually best realized by triathletes and casual competitors and exercisers for whom performance in one particular sport or physical activity is not their uppermost goal.

Why is a single aerobic exercise not sufficient for overall fitness?
As far as conditioning your heart is concerned, one aerobic exercise is
adequate. The benefits that your cardiovascular system receives from
any aerobic exercise are all-purpose: With training, your heart will
pump a larger volume of blood with each contraction, your blood
vessels will be better able to carry this increased supply, and more
blood will go to the lungs, allowing more oxygenated blood to reach
the muscles. This so-called training effect happens regardless of the
kind of aerobic exercise you do.

However, exercise is very specific in what is called its peripheral
effects, which are structural changes that enable the muscles being
exercised to use more oxygen to produce energy. The mitochondria
— the energy factories within cells — increase in number and efficiency, the muscles develop more capillaries, so that more blood
flows into them, and there are changes in the activity of enzymes that
make the biochemical processes involved in metabolism more efficient. While any endurance exercise can improve cardiovascular conditioning, each activity works to develop different, specific sets of
peripheral muscles.

So how do you gauge your level of fitness?
There is no single, precise measure of fitness. If you are well trained
in a particular exercise, your VO_2max, which is a measure of how
much oxygen your body can take in and process during one minute of
intense activity, will be very high when you are performing that particular exercise. However, your VO_2max will be significantly lower
when you perform a sport or exercise you have not trained for. Even
though your heart and lungs are perfectly capable of taking in and
delivering the same volume of oxygen, the untrained muscles that
require the oxygen have a lower capacity to process it than trained
muscles do.

The limitations that peripheral muscles place upon measuring endurance is shown in several studies. For example, a group of subjects
who rode stationary bicycles for eight weeks improved their VO_2max
by 7.8 percent — but when the subjects walked on a treadmill, they
showed only a 2.6 percent improvement. In another study, 15 men
trained intensively at swimming and raised their VO_2max by 11 percent; when they were measured while running on a treadmill, they
showed no improvement when compared with their pretraining rates.
For this reason, VO_2max is not always the best way to measure a
person's fitness. Another aspect of how well you can perform a particular endurance exercise is your anaerobic threshold, which has
become an important component of training for endurance athletes.

What is the anaerobic threshold?
It is the point at which your body shifts from relying on aerobic
metabolism — the oxygen-dependent energy system that sustains endurance exercise — to anaerobic metabolism, which supplies energy

for short bursts of intense effort without using oxygen. Anaerobic metabolism cannot be sustained for longer than a few minutes; therefore, raising your anaerobic threshold allows you to exert yourself more strenuously while still meeting your muscles' energy demands aerobically, so that you can continue a particular sport or activity for longer periods than before.

Anaerobic threshold is related to VO_2max, though the relationship for each person depends on his level of conditioning as well as the speed and duration of the exercise (*see chart, page 21*). An untrained person might reach his anaerobic threshold at 50 percent of his VO_2max, while a well-conditioned person might be able to exercise at 80 percent of his VO_2max and still not reach his anaerobic threshold.

Researchers have charted this relationship by measuring the build-up of lactic acid, a chemical by-product of anaerobic metabolism that accumulates in the muscles and bloodstream and is associated with fatigue during exercise. Studies of trained and untrained subjects indicate that during light and moderate levels of exercise, the lactic acid level in the blood remains fairly constant for both groups. But as exercise becomes intense, untrained subjects exhibit a build-up of lactic acid sooner than trained subjects do, whose lactic acid levels do increase, but at a higher percentage of their VO_2max. Similarly, a high anaerobic threshold accounts for the superior performance of top-ranked endurance athletes, who can work more intensely — and therefore maintain higher speeds — than their less fit competitors without becoming exhausted.

The existence of the anaerobic threshold explains why a runner who is quite fit can quickly become exhausted when he starts swimming laps or pedaling a bicycle; the lack of conditioning in the peripheral muscles permits more lactic acid to accumulate than running at the same oxygen cost would. In trying to increase your overall fitness, therefore, you should focus part of your training regimen on boosting your anaerobic threshold for a variety of activities — a strategy that need not involve more training time and that can make workouts more challenging.

How can you raise your anaerobic threshold?
Raising your anaerobic threshold depends on improving the conditioning of a particular type of skeletal muscle fiber. Skeletal muscles are made of two types of fibers: fast twitch and slow twitch. Fast-twitch fibers, which contract rapidly, depend mostly on anaerobic metabolism for energy. Slow-twitch fibers, which contract at about half the speed of the fast-twitch type, utilize energy that comes from aerobic metabolism.

When you walk or jog or perform any other light exercise, your nervous system recruits mainly the slow-twitch (also called slow-oxidative) fibers to sustain this work. These capillary-rich fibers are slow to fatigue and so are well suited for endurance activities. If you concentrate on long slow distance training — when you exercise steadily at the low end of your target heart rate for a long time — you utilize the slow-twitch fibers. This kind of training will not raise your anaerobic threshold.

The larger but more easily fatigued fast-twitch fibers are called into use when you intensify your effort. These fast-twitch fibers can be further divided into two subsets: fast-oxidative-glycolytic (type A) and fast-glycolytic (type B). The type-A fibers are recruited when you pick up speed — going from jogging to running, for example — and the type-B fibers supply the surge of contractile power needed for sudden bursts of activity like an all-out sprint. Type-A fibers must be exercised to raise your anaerobic threshold, since they utilize some aerobic as well as anaerobic energy; to exercise them, you must work close to but not above your anaerobic threshold. Research has shown that the closer you approach your anaerobic threshold when you work out, the more effectively you will be able to raise it. The chapters on swimming and bicycling in this book include workouts to raise your anaerobic threshold, using interval training and sprints to accomplish this goal.

Can training change the proportion of your fast-twitch to slow-twitch muscle fibers?

This is unlikely. Although there is some evidence that your type-B fast-twitch fibers, which are dependent on anaerobic metabolism almost entirely, can be converted into type-A fast-twitch fibers with training, there is no evidence that fast-twitch fibers can become slow-twitch fibers, and vice versa.

There is a tremendous variation in the distribution of fiber types among individuals, and one person can even have different proportions from muscle to muscle. The average person has 45 to 50 percent slow-twitch fibers, but the relative proportions of your fiber types are determined by your heredity. Training enhances the performance of both types of muscle fibers.

How much should you train?

The amount of training required to build and maintain cardiovascular fitness is well known: three weekly exercise sessions lasting a minimum of a half hour (including 20 minutes of activity at your target heart rate and five minutes each of warm-up and cool-down). How much you must train to build your peripheral conditioning, however, varies with the results you hope to achieve, how much time you can devote to exercise, and the condition you are in. A recent survey of triathletes found that while the serious competitor might train for several hours every day, most participants log in short distances frequently, scheduling their workouts whenever it is possible to fit them into their daily lives.

In fact, most exercise physiologists now believe that the quality of your training matters more than the quantity. For example, swimmers have discovered that interval training, in which you swim

Despite the triathlon's "Ironman" image, most people who enter triathlons do so for recreation, according to a recent survey of participants. The vast majority — 58 percent — said they were swimming, biking and running for fitness, while 33 percent described their motivation as competition, and another 9 percent were considering becoming competitive triathletes. The primary sports background of 52 percent of all these athletes was running; 22 percent were swimmers and 10 percent were cyclists. Fully 83 percent of the triathletes were male, and their average age was 35. The female participants were slightly younger at 32.

Anaerobic Threshold and Performance

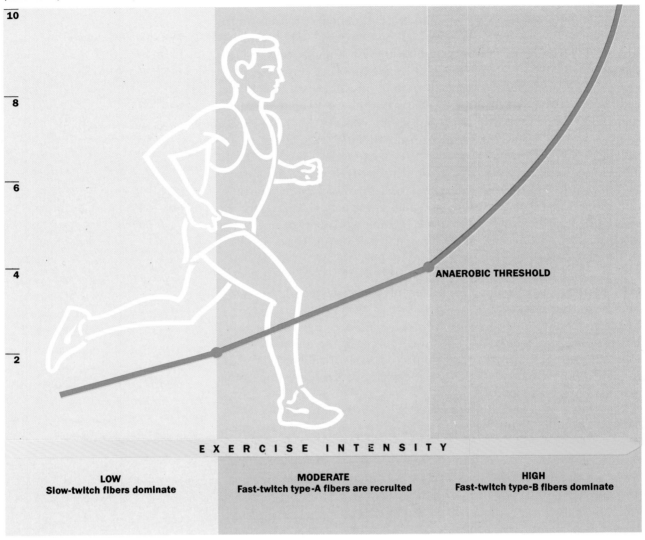

**Lactic acid
(millimoles per liter of blood)**

10

8

6

4 — ANAEROBIC THRESHOLD

2

EXERCISE INTENSITY

LOW
Slow-twitch fibers dominate

MODERATE
Fast-twitch type-A fibers are recruited

HIGH
Fast-twitch type-B fibers dominate

When exercise intensifies, your body's anaerobic system must meet the extra energy demand — a process that results in the production of lactic acid. The point at which lactic acid begins to build up in the bloodstream — followed quickly by fatigue — is called the anaerobic threshold. With training, you can raise the metabolic capacity of one type of fast-twitch fiber, which depends on anaerobic metabolism almost entirely. This will raise your anaerobic threshold, allowing you to increase your effort without fatigue.

relatively short distances with rest intervals in between each stretch, can build their aerobic endurance faster than merely swimming endless laps at a slow, steady pace. (*For information on interval training in swimming, see page 35.*) Likewise, runners can use intervals to work on speed without exhausting themselves: A four-minute mile is impossible for most people, but you can alternate running at this speed for 15 seconds at a time, with 30-second rest periods after each sprint. If you train in this way for a total of 11 minutes and 30 seconds, you will accomplish the equivalent of a four-minute mile.

How can you tell if you are overtraining?

Part of any good training program is allowing adequate time for rest and recovery. Excessive training, especially high-intensity workouts day after day without periodic easy days, can be as much of a problem as insufficient training, paradoxically leading to increasingly poor performance and an actual loss of conditioning. Many well-motivated athletes encounter this problem, which occurs when the body's adaptive mechanisms have been stressed to the point of failure. There are a number of warning signals that may indicate overtraining: weight loss, joint and muscle pain in the absence of injury, nausea, colds and constant fatigue. Women may experience menstrual irregularities.

If you suspect that you might be overtraining, rest for a few days. In severe cases, a break of a week or more might even be necessary. When you return to your training program, work out at a lower intensity or for a shorter time than you had been until you are certain that you have recuperated.

Is the ability to cross train limited by your age?

You can engage in endurance exercises regardless of your age. Active endurance athletes often reach their prime in their late twenties and early thirties — and many recreational exercisers and triathletes are older. The general rule in endurance sports is that the longer the event, the greater the edge older athletes may have, assuming they are as well trained as the younger competitors. This edge depends on the older athletes' having trained consistently over the years. A recent survey of triathletes found that the average age of the men was 35, and the women, 32.

Do you have to be an "iron man" to cross train?

Not anymore. The phrase comes from the Hawaiian triathlon called the Ironman, which when staged in 1978 initially was the first major event of its kind. This race is aptly named: Competitors swim 2.4 miles in open water, then cycle 112 miles, and finish with a 26.2-mile marathon. Today, with more and more people attracted to the sport, shorter triathlons far outnumber events as difficult as the Ironman. Chapter Four provides a training program that will put you in shape for a short triathlon. Chapters Two and Three provide swimming and cycling techniques that can be applied to triathlon training, or to whatever type of cross training you perform. The following pages will guide you toward developing an effective, manageable training program in swimming, cycling and running.

H*ow much exercise is enough — and how much is too much? Scientists have calculated that expending 2,000 calories a week is the optimal rate for substantial fitness returns. This is equivalent to either running 18 miles a week, biking five and a half hours or swimming laps for three hours. Increasing the amount of exercise can continue to provide physiological benefits, up to burning 6,000 calories per week; working out more than that, however, has not been proved to yield additional benefits.*

How to Design Your Own Program

You need not adopt a rigorous program of swimming, cycling and running in order to cross train for fitness. A more casual program, in which you supplement your primary fitness activity with an additional endurance sport, will also give you some of the benefits of cross training. Use the questions at right to determine which kind of cross training will suit you best.

Should you cross train?

1 **Are you bored or otherwise dissatisfied with your current exercise regimen?**

Even the most avid fitness enthusiasts can find that after months or years of performing one activity, their routine becomes monotonous and their fitness gains reach a plateau. If this has happened to you, you may find challenges and new conditioning benefits by expanding your fitness program to include one or more additional activities. You can incorporate cross training into your life informally — letting the seasons guide you, for example, by adding cross-country skiing in the winter, swimming in the summer or cycling in the fall. Or you might decide to challenge yourself with a more rigorous plan in preparation for a triathlon.

2 **Are you fit enough for cross training?**

If you are just beginning a fitness regimen, you would be wise to stay with one sport until you are fairly well conditioned. Performing two (or more) types of exercise will stress more muscle groups, thereby contributing to additional muscle soreness until your body adapts. Also, it will take longer to master the skills involved in each activity if you alternate between them constantly. Get into shape by exercising in one sport three times a week, at a half hour per workout, and at a sufficient intensity to keep your heart in its target range for 20 minutes. Once you can do this comfortably, you can embark on a program of cross training.

As your oxygen-delivery system improves, you can gradually start increasing the intensity and duration of your workouts — or you can add different activities. Bear in mind that you will not be able to perform a new exercise at the same intensity as the ones you have practiced for a long time. Always proceed slowly, at a maximum weekly increase of 10 percent more workout time or intensity. Going faster than this can place undue strain on your muscles and lead to injury.

3 **Have you suffered several exercise-related injuries in the past year?**

If you have had more than one injury serious enough to keep you from working out for several days at a time, it is possible that your current exercise routine is stressing your musculoskeletal system. This is especially true if your injuries tend to recur in the same areas — if you have problems with your knees continually, for example, or if you are sidelined by shin splints repeatedly.

Short of acute injuries, such as a sprained ankle, most sports-related injuries are the result of an overuse syndrome that is due to repeated stress on one body part. Since different sports are powered by different muscle groups, you can reduce the incidence of overuse injuries by performing additional sports that strengthen previously undeveloped muscles. This will distribute the musculoskeletal stress more evenly throughout your body.

4 Is one form of endurance exercise better than another?

The three most common activities used for cross training are swimming, running and cycling. Each sport makes specific demands on the musculoskeletal system and requires different skills. Swimming is the least demanding physiologically, both because of the cushioning effect of the water and your horizontal position in it — which makes it easier for your cardiovascular system to pump blood to the muscles. However, swimming is a most demanding activity in terms of technique. It can take several years for a nonswimmer to develop optimal technical skills — such as those demonstrated in Chapter Two — and neuromuscular coordination.

Running, by comparison, is a fairly simple activity to master, but the physiological effect of repeated pounding places great amounts of stress on your joints and muscles. Also, trainers have noticed that correcting runners' technical errors is more difficult than remedying swimmers' inefficient techniques. This may be because you learn to run as a child, so any problem with your technique is part of a long-established neurological pattern.

Cycling, demonstrated in Chapter Three, can be categorized between the two extremes: It is less demanding physiologically than running and less complex technically than swimming.

5 How much time can you devote to training?

If you have an hour a day, four days a week, that you can devote to exercise, you can incorporate cross training into your life. You can simply alternate sports in a pattern of your own design. A more challenging training regimen that prepares you for a triathlon requires somewhat more time — up to 12.5 hours per week. Such a program appears on page 109.

Most coaches and athletes now believe that the quality of training counts as much as the quantity. This means that you should experiment with shorter-distance intervals, hill work and drills, such as those shown in the following chapters. To guard against overtraining, always take one day off per week; rest is an integral part of any good training program.

How hard should you work out?

The chapters that follow illustrate basic techniques for swimming and cycling that you can use to develop a well-rounded, varied program in each activity. You can also use the charts on the following four pages to determine your training pace and plan a regimen that raises your anaerobic threshold and builds endurance for long distance.

If you decide to challenge yourself by competing in a triathlon, you can use Chapter Four to help you prepare for it. Use the sample nine-week training program on pages 108-109 to reach your personal best for triathlon competition.

Setting Your Pace

Whether you are cross training for a triathlon or simply for fitness, maximizing your training requires that you develop both your aerobic and anaerobic capacities. Aerobic distance work, in which you exercise at 60 to 85 percent of your VO_2max for at least 20 minutes, is your primary training emphasis. However, a good program also includes anaerobic threshold training, and sprint or speed training, in which you work out at 75 to 90 percent for anaerobic threshold training and 100 to 120 percent of your VO_2max for sprint training.

To determine your proper pace range for the various modes of training, you should know your VO_2max. While laboratory testing is necessary for a precise determination of this figure, your maximum heart rate in an all-out time trial for the distances at right will give your approximate heart rate at your VO_2max, to within plus or minus 5 percent.

Perform the time trials for each sport on separate days after an adequate warm-up. Because the distances are relatively short, you should sustain 100 percent intensity for each trial. Immediately after you finish, note the time elapsed and determine your heart rate; record both of these figures in the chart at right, which should be your maximum heart rate.

Use your time for each trial to determine your pace in the chart at right. Then turn to pages 20-21 to correlate your VO_2max pace with the appropriate pace range for each activity. Every six weeks, perform another time trial in each event to assess your development and modify your training as your pace and heart rate improve. (A strengthened, trained heart pumps a greater volume of blood with every contraction than an untrained heart. Therefore, you will find yourself needing to increase your training pace as your heart becomes stronger in order to reach your maximum heart rate.)

Your Personal Time Trial

	Distance	Time	Heart rate/min.	Pace
SWIMMING	500 yards	_____	_____	_____
CYCLING	2 miles	_____	_____	_____
RUNNING	1 mile	_____	_____	_____

Pace Chart

SWIMMING		CYCLING		RUNNING	
Total Time	**Min./100 yd.**	**Total Time**	**MPH**	**Total Time**	**Min./mi.**
10:50	2:10	8:40	15	11:00	11:00
10:00	2:00	7:30	16	10:00	10:00
9:10	1:50	7:04	17	9:00	9:00
8:20	1:40	6:40	18	8:00	8:00
7:30	1:30	6:20	19	7:45	7:45
7:05	1:25	6:00	20	7:30	7:30
6:40	1:20	5:44	21	7:15	7:15
6:15	1:15	5:28	22	7:00	7:00
5:50	1:10	5:14	23	6:45	6:45
5:25	1:05	5:00	24	6:30	6:30
5:00	1:00	4:48	25	6:15	6:15
4:35	0:55	4:36	26	6:00	6:00
		4:26	27	5:45	5:45
		4:16	28	5:30	5:30
		4:08	29	5:15	5:15
		4:00	30	5:00	5:00

SETTING YOUR PACE
(continued)

DISTANCE TRAINING (60-85% VO_2max)					
SWIMMING		**CYCLING**		**RUNNING**	
Time Trial Pace	Training Pace	Time Trial Pace	Training Pace	Time Trial Pace	Training Pace
Min./100 yd.		MPH		Min./mi.	
2:10	3:36-2:33	15	9.0-12.8	11:00	18:20-12:56
2:00	3:20-2:21	16	9.6-13.6	10:00	16:40-11:46
1:50	3:03-2:09	17	10.2-14.4	9:00	15:00-10:35
1:40	2:46-1:57	18	10.8-15.3	8:00	13:20-9:24
1:30	2:30-1:46	19	11.4-16.2	7:45	12:55-9:07
1:25	2:21-1:40	20	12.0-17.0	7:30	12:30-8:49
1:20	2:13-1:34	21	12.6-17.8	7:15	12:05-8:31
1:15	2:05-1:28	22	13.2-18.7	7:00	11:40-8:14
1:10	1:56-1:22	23	13.8-19.6	6:45	11:15-7:56
1:05	1:48-1:16	24	14.4-20.4	6:30	10:50-7:38
1:00	1:40-1:10	25	15.0-21.3	6:15	10:25-7:21
0:55	1:31-1:04	26	15.6-22.1	6:00	10:00-7:03
		27	16.2-23.0	5:45	9:35-6:46
		28	16.8-23.8	5:30	9:10-6:28
		29	17.4-24.6	5:15	8:45-6:10
		30	18.0-25.5	5:00	8:20-5:53

ANAEROBIC THRESHOLD TRAINING
(75-90% VO_2max)

SWIMMING		CYCLING		RUNNING	
Time Trial Pace	Training Pace	Time Trial Pace	Training Pace	Time Trial Pace	Training Pace
Min./100 yd.		MPH		Min./mi.	
2:10	2:53-2:24	15	11.2-13.5	11:00	14:40-12:13
2:00	2:40-2:13	16	12.0-14.4	10:00	13:20-11:06
1:50	2:26-2:02	17	12.8-15.3	9:00	12:00-10:00
1:40	2:13-1:51	18	13.5-16.2	8:00	10:40-8:53
1:30	2:00-1:40	19	14.2-17.1	7:45	10:20-8:36
1:25	1:53-1:34	20	15.0-18.0	7:30	10:00-8:20
1:20	1:46-1:29	21	15.8-18.9	7:15	9:40-8:03
1:15	1:40-1:23	22	16.5-19.8	7:00	9:20-7:46
1:10	1:33-1:17	23	17.2-20.7	6:45	9:00-7:30
1:05	1:26-1:12	24	18.0-21.6	6:30	8:40-7:13
1:00	1:20-1:06	25	18.8-22.5	6:15	8:20-6:56
0:55	1:13-1:01	26	19.5-23.4	6:00	8:00-6:40
		27	20.2-24.3	5:45	7:40-6:23
		28	21.0-25.2	5:30	7:20-6:06
		29	21.8-26.1	5:15	7:00-5:50
		30	22.5-27.0	5:00	6:40-5:33

SPRINT TRAINING
(100-120% VO_2max)

SWIMMING		CYCLING		RUNNING	
Time Trial Pace	Training Pace	Time Trial Pace	Training Pace	Time Trial Pace	Training Pace
Min./100 yd.		MPH		Min./mi.	
2:10	2:10-1:48	15	15.0-18.0	11:00	11:00-9:10
2:00	2:00-1:40	16	16.0-19.2	10:00	10:00-8:20
1:50	1:50-1:31	17	17.0-20.4	9:00	9:00-7:30
1:40	1:40-1:23	18	18.0-21.6	8:00	8:00-6:40
1:30	1:30-1:15	19	19.0-22.8	7:45	7:45-6:27
1:25	1:25-1:10	20	20.0-24.0	7:30	7:30-6:15
1:20	1:20-1:06	21	21.0-25.2	7:15	7:15-6:02
1:15	1:15-1:02	22	22.0-26.4	7:00	7:00-5:50
1:10	1:10-0:58	23	23.0-27.6	6:45	6:45-5:37
1:05	1:05-0:54	24	24.0-28.8	6:30	6:30-5:25
1:00	1:00-0:50	25	25.0-30.0	6:15	6:15-5:12
0:55	0:55-0:46	26	26.0-31.2	6:00	6:00-5:00
		27	27.0-32.4	5:45	5:45-4:47
		28	28.0-33.6	5:30	5:30-4:35
		29	29.0-34.8	5:15	5:15-4:22
		30	30.0-36.0	5:00	5;00-4:10

Keeping Track

An accurate training log is, in reality, a progress report that can help you evaluate and improve your training and performance significantly. As shown in the diary at right, which you can photocopy for repeated use, a log need not be complex. Simply keep a daily record of your training: the kind of workout — distance, sprint or anaerobic threshold — the amount of exercise and how long it took to complete. In addition, record how you felt about your workout.

As important as these quantitative measures are, your comments on how you felt during the workout, both physically and psychologically, are equally vital for evaluating the effectiveness of your program. Were you tired? Were you coping with any injuries? Has your diet changed? Make a note of anything that might affect your progress, such as a cold or even a negative emotional reaction. Then use this information to measure how your training program suits your needs, and if you should alter it.

WEEKLY TRAINING DIARY

Date		Distance Training	Anaerobic Threshold Training	Sprint Training	Comments
Su	SWIMMING				
	CYCLING				
	RUNNING				
M	SWIMMING				
	CYCLING				
	RUNNING				
Tu	SWIMMING				
	CYCLING				
	RUNNING				
W	SWIMMING				
	CYCLING				
	RUNNING				
Th	SWIMMING				
	CYCLING				
	RUNNING				
F	SWIMMING				
	CYCLING				
	RUNNING				
Sa	SWIMMING				
	CYCLING				
	RUNNING				

Weekly Totals

SWIMMING	_____	_____	_____
CYCLING	_____	_____	_____
RUNNING	_____	_____	_____

O ne of the greatest benefits of cross training is that it allows you to develop more muscle groups than any single exercise can. For example, running develops your hamstrings primarily, while cycling focuses more on your quadriceps. By training in both sports, you will balance this overall muscle development.

However, such total body training means your warm-ups must be equally comprehensive. The stretches shown here and on the following six pages will enhance your flexibility in the muscles used for swimming, cycling and running. Even if you alternate workouts on different days, you should do the complete routine, since it will benefit muscle groups that complement one another, and so reduce the chance of injury.

Sit erect with your hands at your sides, your toes pointed and legs outstretched in front of you *(top)*. Slowly bend forward from the waist, tucking your head and reaching for your ankles. Hold for at least 30 seconds. Return to the starting position; repeat two to three times.

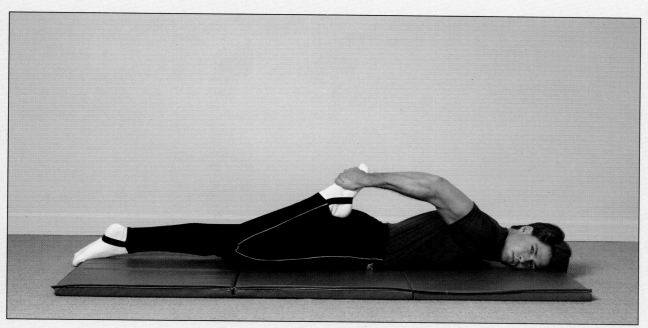

Lie flat on your stomach. Bend your right knee and reach behind you with your right arm, grasping your foot *(above)*. Hold for 30 seconds, lower and switch legs; repeat two to three times.

Sit with your left leg straight and your right leg crossed over it. Wrap your arms around your knee and pull it toward you *(above)*. Repeat two to three times; switch legs.

Conditioners/2

Sit with your back straight, your legs spread and your hands resting on the floor in front of you *(top)*. Slide your hands toward your feet as you bend forward from the waist, leading with your chest *(above)*. Hold for 30 seconds; repeat two to three times.

From a sitting position, bend your knees and press the soles of your feet together. Grasp your ankles, and pull your feet toward you as far as possible *(above)*. Hold for 30 seconds; repeat two to three times.

Stand in front of a wall at arm's length, and press your hands against it at about shoulder height. Bend your left knee forward and stretch your right leg out behind you, pressing both heels to the floor *(above)*. Lean your hips forward slowly. Hold for 30 seconds; switch legs; repeat two to three times.

Stand with your feet shoulder-width apart and your arms at your sides. Stretch your left arm up and over your head and bend to your right side *(above)*. Hold for 10-15 seconds. Return to the starting position; switch sides; repeat two to three times.

From a standing position, raise your right arm and bend it behind your head. Grasp your right elbow with your left hand and pull it gently to the left *(above)*. Hold for 30 seconds; switch arms; repeat the entire sequence two times.

29

Lie flat on your stomach with your legs spread and your hands on the mat at your shoulders. Push your upper body off the mat, arching your back and neck and looking toward the ceiling *(above)*. Hold for five to 10 seconds. Return to the starting position; repeat two to three times.

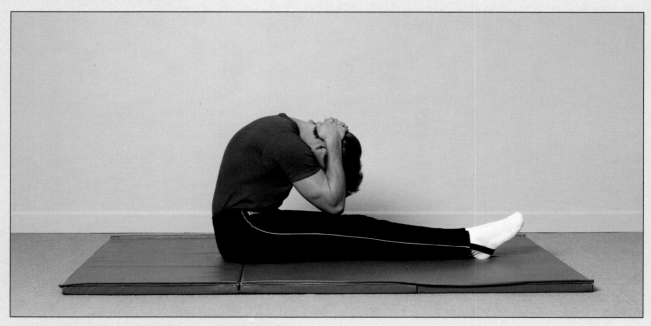

Start in a sitting position with your legs outstretched and toes pointed. Clasp your hands behind your neck and bend forward very gently, stretching your neck as you reach your elbows to your thighs *(above)*. Hold for 15-30 seconds. Return slowly and repeat two to three times.

Lean forward from a kneeling position and reach your left arm
straight out to your right side. Place your right hand on top of
your left, and stretch your upper body away from your hands to
your left *(above)*. Hold for 30 seconds. Return and repeat two
times to each side.

From a kneeling position with your hands on the mat, extend
your right arm out to your right side. Drop your head and
shoulder close to the mat, and stretch to your left *(above)*. You
should feel the stretch in your chest. Hold for 30 seconds;
switch sides; repeat two times.

CHAPTER TWO

Swimming

*Strategies and drills for improving
your speed, endurance and form*

Swimming laps is an excellent cardiovascular conditioner that builds both muscle strength and endurance with minimal risk of injury. Indeed, swimming is essentially the safest endurance activity because you perform it in the cushioning environment of water. However, lap swimming — also called long slow distance swimming — has two potential drawbacks. First, stroking back and forth from one end of a pool to the other can be so boring that many swimmers lose interest quickly. Even more important, swimmers can become discouraged to find that after initial aerobic benefits, their rate of improvement in conditioning, speed and form begins to decline. Adding variety and intensity to your workouts by varying distances, incorporating drills and performing intervals is the best way to invigorate your swimming program and improve your technique.

Distance workouts should form the base of any swimming program. But once you have built an endurance foundation — that is, you can swim continuously for at least 20 minutes within your target heart rate — you can counter the boredom and diminishing returns of swimming laps by varying your exercise program. This is done with interval training — breaking your workout into shorter, faster swims that are interspersed with brief rest periods. (The box on the opposite page describes some of the different ways to employ intervals in your workout routines.)

A typical swimming program that makes use of intervals consists of a slow warm-up swim, a period of interval training and a cool-down swim. Warm-ups generally account for 15 to 25 percent of the total distance; cool-downs should be about 10 percent. Longer warm-ups and cool-downs are advisable for particularly stressful workouts. Another 30 percent of each workout can be devoted to the technical aspects of stroking, kicking and breathing drills, such as those shown on pages 41, 45-46, and 50-51.

One of the best ways to improve a swimming routine is to concentrate each workout on a particular level of effort. The ratios of work intensity or speed, duration and recovery time determine just how aerobic or anaerobic an interval is. A well-rounded swimming program includes short, maximum-effort swims to develop sprinting ability and technique; middle-distance workouts to improve lactic acid tolerance and to increase your anaerobic threshold; and distance work to build endurance, concentration and a sense of pacing. The length of your rest periods and level of effort used determine whether sprinting ability or lactic acid tolerance is being emphasized: The farther your heart rate drops between swim repeats (the distance you swim without resting), the more your workout emphasizes speed instead of endurance.

In a distance "set," or series of laps, you swim continuously for up to 2,000 yards or more, with rest periods taking only 20 to 25 percent of the total workout time. The object of this kind of program — often called an overdistance workout because you swim "over" the distance of most races — is to maintain an elevated heart rate and a steady pace for relatively long periods.

Shorter repeats of less than 200 yards, performed fast enough so your muscles use anaerobic energy, are typical of middle-distance swimming. Because your pace is faster than it would be in an overdistance workout, you require more substantial periods of rest between swims. A typical middle-distance swim would consist of 200 yards at an easy pace, followed by a 30-second rest, then 200 yards at a faster pace, followed by a 20-second rest, and a final 200 yards at your fastest pace.

While the main goal of sprint training is to increase your speed, it also enhances stroke efficiency by improving the neuromuscular coordination of your swimming. Even if you do not want to become the fastest swimmer in your pool, you can enhance your technique by including sprint swims in your workout. Short, fast swims that raise your heart rate quickly to or above your target zone build sprinting

Interval Training

◆ When you perform intervals, each distance you swim without stopping is called a repeat; groups of repeats are called sets. For example, if you were to swim repeats of 100 yards in a 25-yard pool, you would swim the length of the pool four times without a rest for each repeat.

◆ Intervals are expressed as the number of swims times the length of the swim times the amount of time between departures. You might decide to swim 10 × 100 × 1:45, which would mean swimming 10 repeats of 100 yards, beginning each swim 1 minute and 45 seconds after the previous one. The faster you swim each set, the longer you can rest during each interval.

◆ You can swim decreasing interval sets, in which you shorten the interval for each swim. For example, you could swim your first three of 10 swims in 1 minute and 45 seconds, the next three in 1:30 and the next in 1:15. You could follow this last group with an extra long rest and then swim the last repeat as fast as you possibly can.

◆ Another alternative is swimming ladder sets, in which you vary the distances of the repeats. For example, you could swim 50, 100, 150, 200, 250 and 300 yards in a set of six. To calculate the interval for each repeat, you can use a constant rest interval — of 30 seconds, for instance — between every interval swim.

ability. Because moving very quickly into this high-performance zone is stressful, you must take relatively long rests between sprints at first, with the rest periods lasting considerably longer than the swim times. A typical sprint lasts less than 10 seconds; a typical rest lasts at least twice that long. The distance you swim for this type of training should be between 15 and 100 yards.

Incorporating these various strategies into a typical week of training, you might include one session of distance training, two or three sessions of middle-distance training and a session or two of sprinting, alternating the workouts to minimize boredom. For most swimmers, it is a good idea to establish technique and endurance before working on speed. Paying attention to your technique is especially important because minor lapses in swimming form are common, even among experienced swimmers, and such mistakes can be more costly than faults in running or cycling technique, since the resistance of water is so much greater than wind resistance. The following pages not only demonstrate the most efficient form for performing the freestyle swimming stroke — the stroke most often used for endurance swimming — but also show you mistakes that swimmers are most likely to make. You will also find drills to help you perfect your form. Work on some aspect of your form at every workout; this helps to make the exercise more challenging, and you will be rewarded with small but steady improvements.

Streamlining

The hydrodynamics of swimming are based on principles similar to the aerodynamics of flying: An object that is flatter and more streamlined will move through either water or air faster than an angled object, which catches more resistance. A flat, streamlined swimming position creates relatively little disruption of the water. This means you will encounter less resistance — called drag — to hold you back, and require less energy for forward momentum.

Proper body alignment, shown on these two pages, is probably the most essential element of good swimming form, since effective stroke mechanics, kicking form and breathing techniques all stem from it. Your body should be streamlined both horizontally and laterally. Horizontal streamlining will keep you flat and shallow in the water so that you encounter minimum resistance to forward motion. Aligning your body laterally will keep it in a straight line so that it does not fishtail from side to side, which increases resistance by presenting a greater body area to the water. (In this chapter, common mistakes in body position, stroking and other aspects of form are shown in black-and-white photographs.)

For lateral streamlining, your head, shoulders, hips and feet should be aligned *(above)*. When stroking, your body should twist as a unit; avoid side-to-side swaying. Kicking helps to counterbalance the rolling caused by your arm stroke.

To streamline your body horizontally, keep it as flat as possible in the water. Your head should be lowered so it breaks the water at about your hairline, your back level and your feet and legs near the water's surface *(above)*.

WRONG Inclining your body at a diagonal to the water's surface *(right)* leads to inefficient swimming. Your hips and legs are sunken at a downward angle, while your head is high, which increases lateral resistance as you swim.

Stroking Mechanics

ost of the momentum of swimming comes from your stroke. On these and the following 10 pages, the crawl, or freestyle, stroke — the most frequently used stroke of both fitness and competitive swimmers — is broken into its component parts and accompanied by typical errors and corrective drills. Taking time to learn the elements of your stroke and to analyze it will improve your swimming efficiency markedly.

The freestyle stroke can be divided into three phases, starting with the entry phase — the beginning of the stroke in which the hand first enters the water. This phase concludes with the catch, when the hand, now underwater, first applies pressure to the water. The power phase, which includes the pull, push and finish, shown on pages 42-47, actually moves the water backward to provide the stroke's forward momentum. Finally, in the recovery phase, demonstrated on pages 48-49, the hand and arm leave the water behind you and then circle forward through the air to prepare for the next stroke cycle.

Although the three stroke phases are examined independently, it is important to remember that they are interrelated: Effective stroking is contingent on both a proper entry and recovery. You will most enhance your swimming by perfecting all areas of stroking.

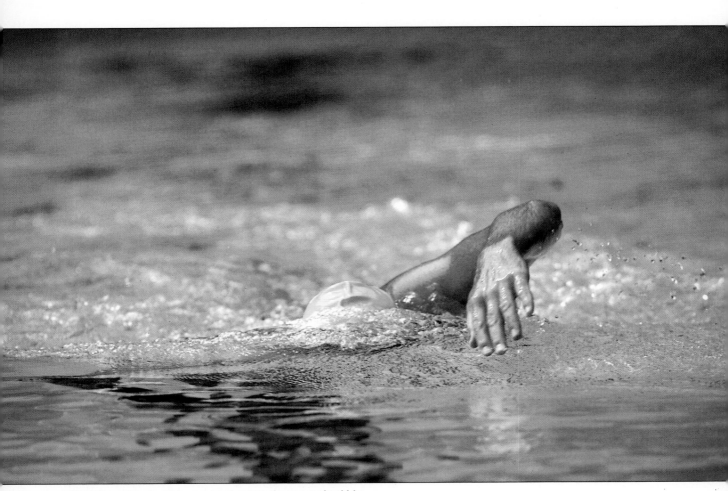

ENTRY The point at which your hand enters the water should be in line with your ear and between nine inches to a foot in front of your head. While your hand is still out of the water, hold your elbow high and bent at almost a 90-degree angle. Keep your palm pitched, or tilted, outward at a 45-degree angle so that your thumb enters the water first *(above)*.

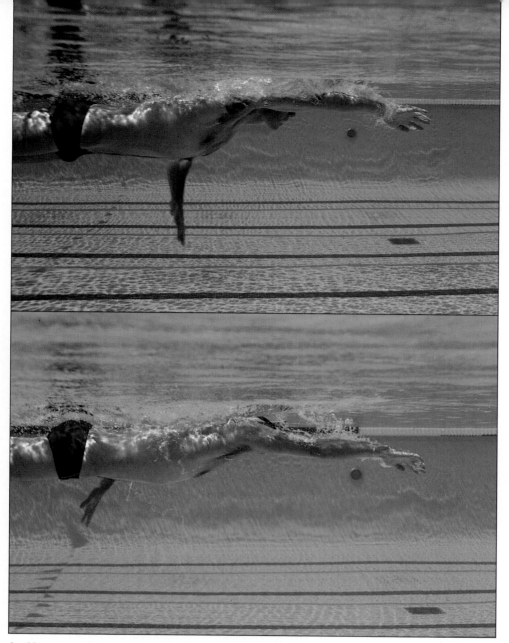

As this underwater view of the entry shows, your hand should lead, with your bent elbow following *(top)*. In a correct entry, the pitch of the hand will allow a minimum of drag-creating bubbles. To prepare for the catch of the entry *(above)*, as you enter the water, extend your elbow and press your hand forward, elevating your shoulder girdle as you push downward gradually to about a foot below the water's surface.

Entry Errors and Drills

WRONG A typical entry mistake is to extend your arm before it enters the water *(right).* This not only strains the muscles of the shoulder and the back, but also traps air bubbles, creates more drag and can hinder proper torso rotation.

WRONG Reaching past the body's center line *(left)* disrupts your lateral alignment by causing your hips and shoulders to turn from side to side excessively. Your arm should not cross in front of your head on entry.

DRILL Exaggerating the point of entry will allow you to both feel and visualize the difference between proper entry and either overextending or overreaching. Instead of entering with your arm about a foot in front of your head, bend your elbow more sharply and push your hand downward into the water like a piston right next to your ear *(above)*. Alternate one lap of drill swimming with one lap of regular swimming for five-to-10 25-yard laps.

The Power
Phase/1

During this part of the stroke, your arm sweeps from the catch position in front of your body to the finish behind you. The force of the power phase is determined largely by the roll of your shoulders and torso, which should rotate upward about 45 degrees as your arm moves past.

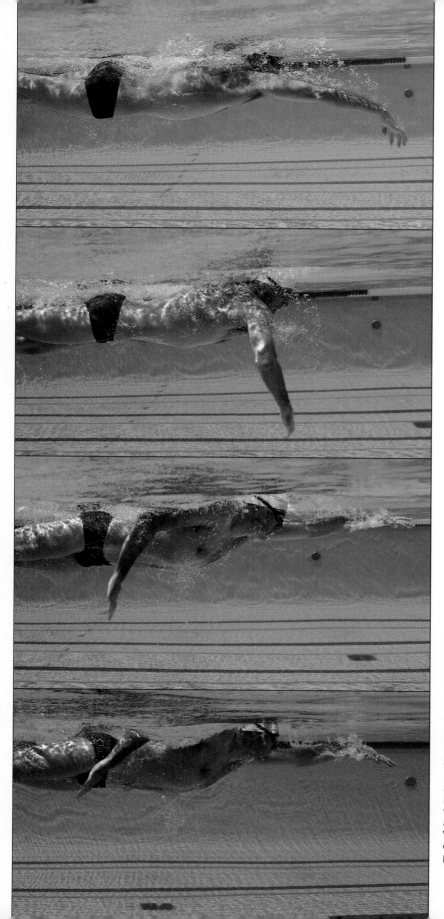

The power phase of the stroke starts with the pull *(top)*, during which you push your hand downward, turning it in toward the center line of your body, and start to bend your elbow. As the pull continues *(second)*, flex your wrist and continue bending your elbow until it reaches a maximum angle of about 90 degrees when your arm is beneath your chest. At this point, begin the push phase *(third)*, by rotating your hand to face almost directly behind you as it pushes the water away. Finally, at the finish *(bottom)*, begin to straighten your elbow as it leaves the water, rotating your palm in toward your thigh as your hand continues to push backward. Your pinky should lead as your hand begins to leave the water. When performing the power phase correctly, you should feel constant pressure on your palms.

43

The Power Phase/2

The correct elbow bend during the power phase *(right)* is crucial if you are to achieve maximum propulsion while swimming. Ideally, you should start bending your elbow immediately after the catch, and it should reach a maximum bend of 90 degrees when it is directly beneath your body. This angle should gradually increase as you continue to push backward.

WRONG The dropped elbow *(right)* is the most serious of all stroking flaws: The elbow is prematurely bent so that it is lower than the hand when entering the water. This wastes energy, since the lowered elbow and shoulder are not in a maximum power position and so cannot move the water effectively. In addition, this incorrect position can lead to shoulder injuries.

WRONG Powering your stroke with a straight elbow *(right)* is also ineffective, since it relies strictly on arm strength for power, and does not allow you to utilize the larger and stronger muscles of your back. Additionally, this stroking flaw can decrease torso rotation and lead to shoulder injuries.

Power Drills

Swimming on your side is a good way to practice the correct rotation of your torso, which will enhance the power phase of your stroke. After completing a normal left-arm stroke cycle, turn onto your right side, extending your right arm underneath your body, and kick 10 times *(right)*. Return to a horizontal position and complete another full stroke cycle, then turn onto your left side and repeat *(bottom)*. Perform this for 25 yards.

A pulling set that works on the propulsive power of your stroke should comprise 10 to 20 percent of your workout. Use flotation devices to keep your legs suspended at the proper height *(above)*, so that all of your momentum comes from your upper body. Insert a pull-buoy between your upper thighs and, optionally, secure your ankles inside a small inner tube.

Recovery

A good recovery provides your arm with a restful transition between the more propulsive entry and power phases. Your elbow should emerge from the water first, with your forearm perpendicular to it *(above)*. Increase your elbow bend as you bring your hand fully out of the water and up along your side *(second)*. Start to extend your forearm, bringing your hand forward in front of your head *(third)*. Finally, swing your whole arm forward as you prepare for another entry phase into the water *(fourth)*.

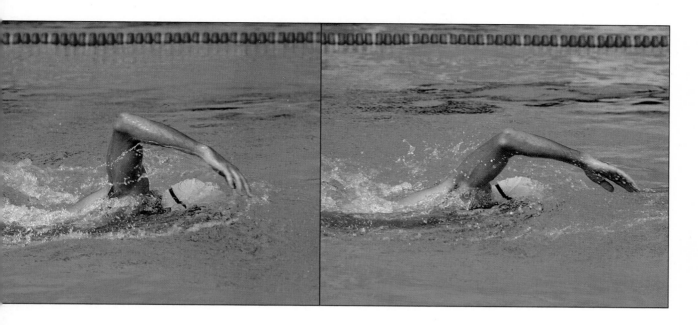

WRONG A wide recovery is a common stroking error in which the arm stays straight and swings outward in a wide arc *(right)*. This can disrupt lateral streamlining, causing you to lose energy. Be sure that your elbow exits the water before your hand, and that it stays bent through the entire recovery.

WRONG The palm of your hand should not show during the recovery *(right)*. The recovery phase should give your arm a chance to relax, and rotating your hand outward creates stress that can cause shoulder injuries.

The Flutter Kick

While the forward momentum of swimming comes almost entirely from the stroking action of your arms, the kick has a crucial function: It prevents your lower body from sinking, helping to maintain streamlining.

The two most typical kick styles are the two-beat and six-beat kicks. In a two-beat kick, the swimmer kicks once with each arm stroke; in the six-beat kick, three times per arm stroke. Generally two-beat kicks plunge a little deeper than the more rapid six-beat kick. There are also less common kick variations, such as the four-beat kick — two kicks per arm stroke — and the two-beat crossover in which the feet actually scissor across each other. Ideally, you will develop your own kicking rhythm after you have perfected your stroke. The kick you use is largely — and best — determined by your particular body mechanics and stroking style.

Whichever beat kick you use, your form should be the same. Keep your toes pointed and your knees almost straight. The kicking action should come from your hips. Your feet should be about a foot apart at the widest point. Do not actually bring your upper foot out of the water completely; rather, your heel should just break the water's surface (above).

WRONG The hooked foot *(above)*, with ankles flexed and toes pointed straight downward, decreases the effectiveness of your kick. Because it is less streamlined, this kicking flaw drags your lower body downward and wastes energy.

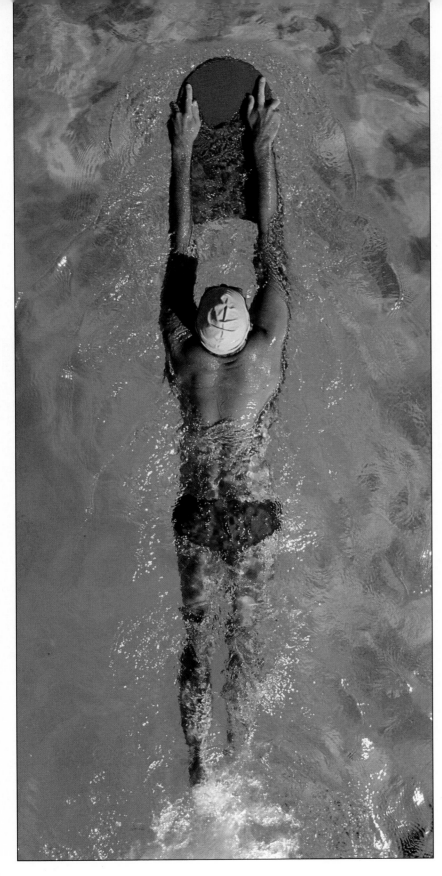

Kicking Drills

Using a kickboard is one of the best ways to perfect your kick as well as to condition your leg muscles. Stretch the board in front of you fully and grasp it on either side just where it begins to round *(left)*. Keep your body aligned, with your shoulders low and your hips near the surface of the water. Spend 10 to 15 percent of your workout on kicking drills.

Another way to practice kicking is on your side. Your lower arm should be fully extended to keep your body up. Power the kick from your hips. Perform this for 25 yards on your left side; repeat the drill on your right side.

Breathing/1

Rhythmic, relaxed breathing is essential to swimming, as it prevents fatigue and aids in stroke mechanics. It should require no more thought than breathing while doing any other physical activity. Quite simply, you should exhale completely through both your mouth and nose while your face is underwater, and inhale through your mouth when your arm begins its recovery. One breath intake per stroke cycle — a right and left arm stroke — is usually adequate for most swimmers.

Determining which side to breathe on is a matter of personal preference, and many experts believe that swimmers should be able to breathe bilaterally, as shown above. Whichever side you breathe on, turn your head into the trough of water, or bow wave, created by your head by your forward momentum. The gap created by the bow wave will allow you more time to inhale.

When breathing bilaterally, take a breath every third arm stroke: As your right arm begins its recovery, take advantage of your body's rolling movement and start turning your neck to the right *(far left)*. When your right arm first leaves the water, turn your head fully to inhale *(second)*. Roll your head back to the center line of your body and exhale as your right arm completes its recovery *(third)*. Keep your head submerged and exhale gradually during a complete left- and right-stroke cycle, then inhale to your left as you begin your recovery *(fourth)*.

WRONG Breathing late in the recovery, or turning your head too far underneath your arm, causes your torso to twist out of lateral alignment, reducing stroke efficiency *(above)*. Avoid this by starting to turn your head when your arm is just beginning its recovery.

Breathing/2

The correct head position assists in breathing and also ensures that optimal streamlining is maintained. When exhaling, your head should be half submerged and your eyes focused downward at about a 45-degree angle *(left)*. As your arm completes its pull and begins its recovery, turn your head to follow the natural roll of your body *(below)*, but continue rotating your neck to allow your mouth and nose to emerge from the water for inhaling.

Strengtheners for Swimmers/1

While swimming strength- ens the upper body pri- marily, it does entail some use of all the body's major muscle groups. Conditioning these muscles through specific strength- ening exercises will allow you to de- velop more power in both your stroke and kick, and to use them more effectively. As a result, you will be able to swim farther and faster without fatigue.

The swim strengtheners demon- strated here and on the following four pages concentrate on the mus- cles of the shoulders, the legs and the abdomen. They are designed to strengthen the primary as well as secondary muscle groups required for swimming. Some of the exercises require weights. Start with two- or three-pound dumbbells or ankle weights. As your strength improves, you can increase the poundage.

Holding dumbbells, stand straight with your feet together and your arms at your sides. Raise your arms out to your sides at shoulder height *(far left)*; lower *(center)*. Raise your arms to shoulder height in front of you *(left)*; lower; perform eight to 15 repetitions.

Place your bent right knee and straight right arm on a weight bench, keeping your back flat. Hold a dumbbell in your left hand and let your arm dangle *(below left)*. Bend your elbow and raise the dumbbell to the side of your torso *(below right)*; lower; perform eight to 15 repetitions; switch arms.

Strengtheners for Swimmers/2

Sit erect with your hands at your sides, your right knee bent and your left leg extended in front of you. Raise your left leg from three inches to a foot off the mat *(above)*; hold momentarily, then lower slowly. Perform 10-20 repetitions; switch legs.

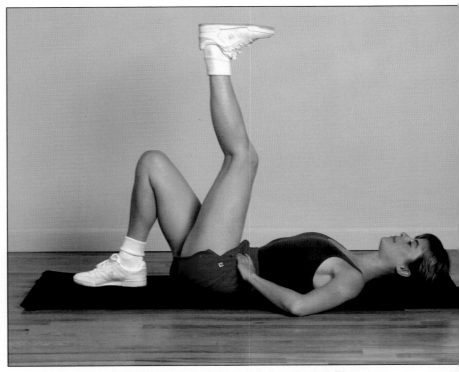

Lie on your back with your right knee bent and your left leg extended. Place your hands on your hips and raise your left leg to be perpendicular to the floor, keeping your knee bent *(above)*. Lower slowly. Repeat 10-20 times; switch legs.

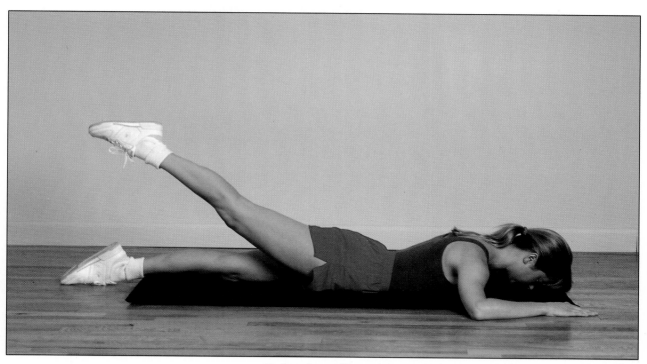

Lie face down with your legs extended and your elbows bent at shoulder level. Keeping your toes pointed, tighten your buttocks while raising your right leg high without arching your back *(above)*; hold for two seconds and lower slowly. Repeat 10-20 times; switch legs.

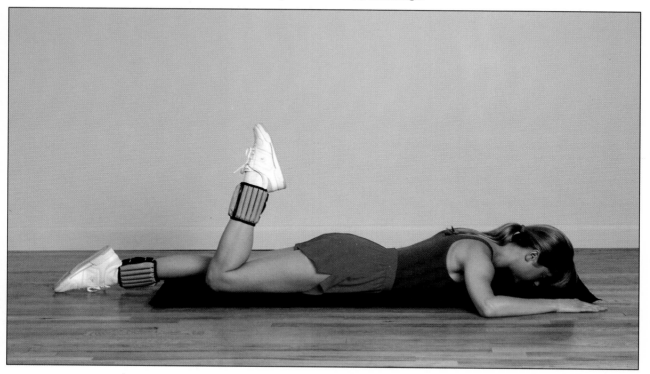

Wear ankle weights and lie face down on a mat with your elbows bent at shoulder level. Bend your right knee and raise your calf, keeping your foot pointed *(above)*. Lower slowly; repeat 10-20 times; switch legs.

Lie on a weight bench with your knees bent, thighs pulled toward your torso and lower back flat. Hold a dumbbell between two hands above your chest with your arms extended and elbows bent slightly *(above left)*. Stretch your arms over your head, letting the weight hang downward *(above right)*. Return to the starting position; repeat eight to 15 times.

Lie on your back with your knees bent and feet flat on the floor, and your arms crossed over your chest *(top)*. Using your abdominals, raise your head, shoulders and upper back *(above)*. Hold momentarily; lower slowly and repeat 10-30 times.

CHAPTER THREE

Cycling

Outdoor conditioning on varied terrain

Cyclists are far more dependent on equipment than are runners or swimmers. Yet, in a sense, cycling is the freest and the most versatile of exercises. You can move with speed, outdoors, on a machine that not only transports you, but is powered by you; you can cover the sweeping distances and the varied terrain that you might travel in an automobile; and you can enjoy this blend of body and machine in a variety of circumstances — cycling on scenic tours alone or with a group, commuting to work, unwinding with a ride at the end of the day or racing.

If you are already an experienced cyclist, you are probably aware of some of the benefits of this sport. Bicycle riding not only tones and strengthens your legs and shoulders, but also helps stretch your lower back, conditioning it for swimming and running. For injured runners, cycling is ideal, since it exercises the leg muscles while imposing far less stress than running. In terms of developing aerobic capacity, cycling can be as effective as running.

In the past few years, the introduction of mountain bikes — also known as all-terrain bikes or ATBs — has extended the enjoyment of biking by letting cyclists traverse trails and slopes that were once inaccessible to them. Indeed, ATBs have become so popular that they now make up half or more of total bicycle sales in some parts of the country. Because these bikes allow better maneuverability and a more upright position than racing or touring bicycles (see page 92), many bicycle commuters have adopted ATBs for city riding.

If you do not have a bicycle, the information on pages 68-69 provides guidelines for choosing one, and explains the major differences between a 10- or 12-speed racing or touring bike, and an ATB. Just as important as choosing a bike is fitting it to your dimensions. In a study at the U.S. Olympic Training Center, racing cyclists increased their cardiovascular efficiency by 8 to 14 percent simply by having their bicycles fitted properly — an effect equivalent to losing 10 pounds of body weight. (See the box on the opposite page.)

Having a bike fit properly is the first step toward feeling comfortable on it; learning to handle it confidently is the next. Indeed, cyclists training for Olympic competition are so relaxed that they can graze one another without falling when they are in the middle of a pack moving at 25 miles per hour. The point of such mastery is not simply to avoid spills, but also to feel at ease so that your energy for forward propulsion is conserved. The riding techniques on the following pages are designed to help keep your upper body and torso movement to a minimum and let your legs do the work.

Because a bicycle is such an efficient machine, it is possible to go for a spin and never reach your target heart rate. If your cardiovascular system is already well conditioned from another aerobic activity, familiarize yourself with cycling by riding on relatively flat terrain for 20 to 30 minutes three times a week for at least two weeks. Begin each ride pedaling in a low gear at a steady 55 to 60 revolutions per minute to warm up; after 10 minutes, increase your cadence to 70 to 80 rpms and shift to a low or medium gear that raises your heart rate into its training zone. Perhaps the most common mistake that novice cyclists make is to pedal in too high a gear, which will not only wear you out quickly, but put undue strain on your knees. Use this initial period to concentrate on high-rpm, low-gear riding and to improve your bike-handling skills.

Over the next two to four weeks, add a fourth cycling day per week and climb some modest hills twice weekly. Try to accomplish a minimum of three rides of 45 to 60 minutes; use weekends for at least one longer, relatively easy ride of 20 to 30 miles. After five or six weeks, your technique should improve considerably and your cadence should be a steady 75 to 90 rpms.

With this conditioning as a base, you should reach the point in your third month of training when you can ride 30 to 40 miles at a time, and be able to increase your weekly mileage by 8 to 10 percent. Add variety to your cycling program by climbing steeper hills or by in-

Fitting Your Bike

For optimal cycling efficiency and comfort, it is crucial that your bike be fitted properly to your body proportions. If you purchase a new bike at a reputable bike shop, the sales personnel will help you make the proper measurements and adjustments. However, with the help of a friend, it is simple to determine the correct size for you by using the following guidelines. (The diagrams on pages 68-69 identify the parts of a bicycle that are referred to below.)

◆ Your first consideration is the frame size itself, which cannot be adjusted. You should know this measurement when you begin examining a bike to make a purchase. Hold the handlebars steady and straddle the top tube so that you are standing flat-footed on the ground in front of the saddle. There should be a one- to two-inch clearance between the top tube and your crotch. Because a smaller frame size is preferable on an ATB, you should allow a clearance of two to three inches.

◆ To determine the appropriate saddle height, have someone hold the handlebars steady while you sit in a comfortable riding position with your hands on the handlebars. When the pedal is at its lowest point, in the six o'clock position, your knee should be bent slightly.

◆ Assessing how far to slide the saddle forward or backward requires the use of a plumb line. Sit in a comfortable riding posture while someone holds the bike steady. Place the pedals at the three o'clock/nine o'clock position. A plumb line held directly behind your kneecap should fall straight past the ball of your foot and down to the pedal axle.

◆ To adjust the height of the handlebars and stem, have someone hold you steady while you sit on the saddle. Position the bars and stem about one to two inches below the bottom of the saddle. For correct stem length, hold one of your elbows against the tip of the saddle, and extend your forearm straight toward the stem. Your middle finger should reach halfway across the length of the stem.

terval training. Your aim should be to increase your heart rate to 80 percent of its maximum for three- to five-minute intervals, followed by rest periods during which you pedal easily in a low gear for five minutes. Repeat this sequence four or five times. Vary the length and intensity of riding intervals, depending on how you feel, but do not overdo them; experienced cyclists generally limit bouts of interval training to twice a week. Mountain biking also provides an ideal opportunity for intervals of intense riding, since trekking over uneven trails makes you work harder than touring over paved roads.

After three months of building your overall stamina, you can train for specific events. Riding a century — a 100-mile ride — calls for increasing your weekly training to at least 140 miles and being able to do two five- or six-hour rides on successive days. For bicycle touring, it is helpful to devote at least two days a week to hill climbing, and also to condition your upper body to handle a bike loaded with packs weighing as much as 30 or 40 pounds. Whatever your biking goals are, you will benefit from learning the riding techniques and conditioning exercises on the following pages.

The Right Bike

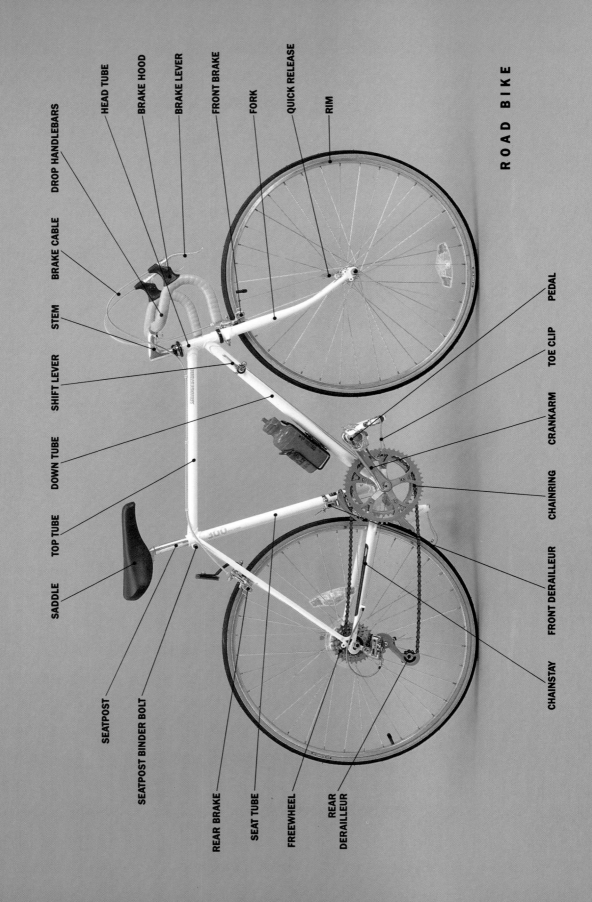

ROAD BIKE

DROP HANDLEBARS
HEAD TUBE
BRAKE HOOD
BRAKE LEVER
FRONT BRAKE
FORK
QUICK RELEASE
RIM

BRAKE CABLE
STEM
SHIFT LEVER
DOWN TUBE
TOP TUBE
SADDLE

SEATPOST
SEATPOST BINDER BOLT

REAR BRAKE
SEAT TUBE
FREEWHEEL
REAR DERAILLEUR

CHAINSTAY
FRONT DERAILLEUR
CHAINRING
CRANKARM
TOE CLIP
PEDAL

SEATPOST QUICK RELEASE

WIDER SADDLE

LARGE-DIAMETER TUBING

UPRIGHT HANDLEBARS

THUMB SHIFTER

CANTILEVER BRAKE

KNOBBY TIRE

NUTTED OR QUICK-RELEASE AXLE

SMALLER FRAME SIZE THAN COMPARABLE ROAD BIKES

PEDAL WITH SOLE GRIPS

LONGER CRANKARM

TRIPLE CHAINRING

U-BRAKE OR ROLLER CAM

VARIABLE-LENGTH CHAINSTAY

LONG-CAGE DERAILLEUR

WIDE-RANGE FREEWHEEL

A L L - T E R R A I N   B I K E

B uying a good bicycle is an investment. To choose wisely, you should be familiar with bike parts and the differences between road or touring and all-terrain bicycles (*above*).

The most apparent differences between these two popular types of bicycles are the smaller, heavier frame sizes, upright handlebars and wider, knobby tires of the ATBs. While these features increase your riding stability and comfort, they also result in less speed potential. Likewise, the cantilever brakes, U-brakes or roller cams found on ATBs are bigger and more powerful than the brakes on road bikes.

ATBs also provide up to 18 gears, which allow you more options and control when climbing steep hills or navigating over rough terrain. Such features are not needed on a road bike used for touring or racing.

The Right Equipment

Bicycle equipment for the dedicated cyclist does not end with the purchase of the bike itself. Having the right cycling accessories can improve your performance as well as increase your riding comfort and safety.

Clockwise from top right: A good helmet is a necessity; it will greatly reduce your risk of injury in the event of a fall. Helmets must pass nationwide safety standards established by the American National Standards Institute (ANSI) or the Snell Memorial Foundation; be sure you choose one with an ANSI or Snell approval sticker. Today's helmets come in both hard-shell and lighter, Styrofoam models, which weigh a little more than seven ounces.

Saddles can be purchased separately to suit your particular riding needs. Gel-filled saddles increase riding comfort greatly by providing extra form-fitting cushioning. A cyclometer, which clips onto your handlebars and measures distance, cadence and time, is a valuable training aid. A water bottle, which attaches to a holder on the bike's downtube, is another essential.

Padded cycling gloves protect your hands from blisters and minimize road shock. Likewise, well-padded cycling shorts have a deerskin or synthetic-lined crotch that absorbs moisture and protects your inner thighs and groin from chafing and saddle sores.

Cycling shoes feature inflexible soles that increase your pedaling efficiency. Experienced riders choose cleated shoes or the latest pedal/shoe systems, shown at top left, which clip directly onto the pedals.

The correct cycling posture shown here demonstrates the importance of stream-lining. Lower your torso by bending forward at the waist, keeping your back parallel to the top tube *(right)*. Your head should be low, with your neck in line with your spine. Keep your elbows flexed slightly and tucked toward your knees.

Body Position

Your position on a bicycle can make a considerable difference in both the effectiveness and comfort of your riding. One study that examined the effects of several variables on speed showed that improved riding position, with a time decrease of four minutes and 31 seconds, accounted for a greater benefit than any other variable.

Proper riding posture begins with an accurate fit of the bike to your body, as shown on page 67. Only after such mechanical adjustments are made can you evaluate your actual riding posture. To achieve an optimal cycling position, consider two dynamics: First, distribute your body weight between the handlebars and the saddle. Weight distribution is dictated by terrain, and can be adjusted by changing your hand positions, as shown on pages 74-75, plus sliding backward or forward on the saddle. Secondly, minimize wind resistance: Research has shown that 90 percent of your cycling energy is expended in pushing air away from you. Thus, the more you streamline your body position by keeping your torso as horizontal as possible, the more effective your riding will be. Not only will you meet much less resistance when you are riding against the wind, you will pick up more speed when riding with it.

Hand Positions

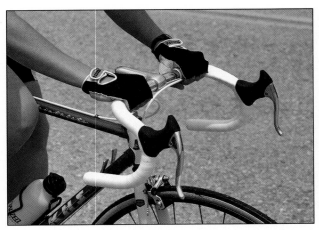

Hold the handlebars near the stem when hill climbing from a seated position or for a rapid, smooth descent with no braking required to slow down.

Resting your hands on the handlebars above the brake levers is ideal for cruising, since it allows you to assume a slightly more upright, relaxed posture.

Grasping the brake hoods provides easy access to the brakes for riding downhill. In this position, you can feather the brakes off and on with your first two fingers.

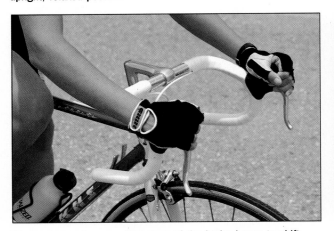

Wrap your hands around the tops of the brake levers to shift your body weight to the front of the bike for out-of-the-saddle uphill climbs.

Place your hands in the dropped part of the handlebars below the brake hoods, which allows easy access to the brake levers, for rapid descents that might require braking.

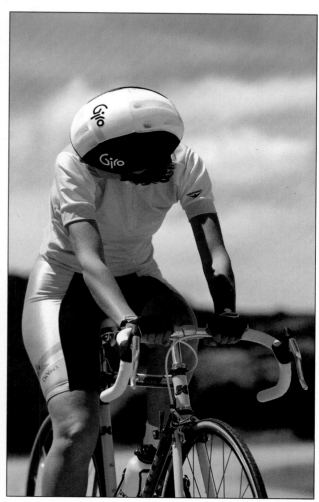

You will frequently need to ride with one hand on the handle-bars, whether to change gears or to grab something to eat from your shirt pocket. Stabilize the bike by moving both hands close to the handlebar stem; then you can steer safely with one hand without losing your balance.

Maintaining a straight line while turning to look behind you is a simple — but necessary — skill, especially when riding in traffic. Keeping your hands close to the handlebar stem, main-tain a straight line by turning your head only, with your body weight centered forward.

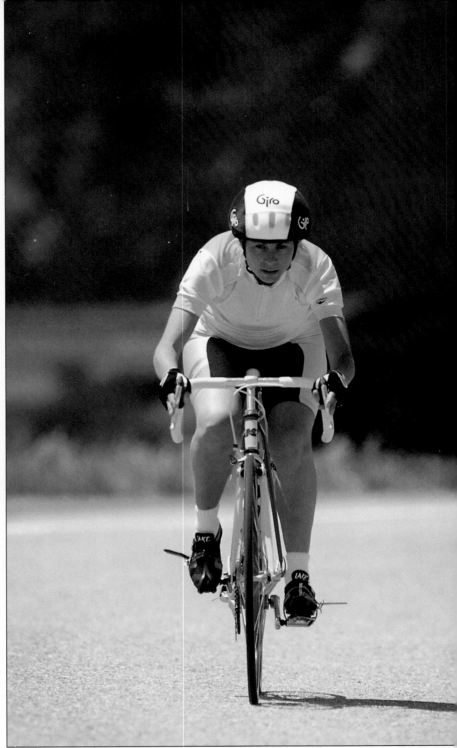

For efficient pedaling, both legs should be in constant motion of equal effort, with your knees tucked in close to the bike *(above).* When one foot is at the 12 o'clock position to begin the downstroke, the other is about to begin the upstroke from the six o'clock position *(top left).* The 12-to-six o'clock downstroke utilizes your quadriceps and shins; the six-to-12 o'clock upstroke works the hamstrings and calves.

Pedaling

Skillful pedaling is probably the most important component of cycling. Novice cyclists often think of pedaling as an up-and-down motion, which is an ineffective way to ride, since it overdevelops some muscles of the leg while underutilizing others. Instead, pedal in a smooth, circular pattern to better distribute the workload throughout the leg muscles. This depends as much on pulling upward on the pedals as it does on pushing downward.

To perform smooth rotations, and make sure that your upward and downward force on the pedals is equal, it is essential that your bike be equipped with toe clips, or that you have cleated shoes that lock into the pedals. Practice inserting your feet in and out of the toe clips so you are prepared to disengage them if you need to stop.

For maximum cycling speed and endurance, your cadence, or pedaling rhythm, should be constant. Cadence is measured in revolutions per minute, or rpms. Strive to pedal between 80 to 90 rpms; with practice, this cadence will become second nature. To determine your cadence, count the complete pedal strokes of one foot for 15 seconds and multiply this number by four.

One-legged pedaling will isolate the pedaling action to strengthen your hip flexors, and thus improve your upstroke. To perform this exercise, put your bike on a windloader, or home trainer, such as the one shown at right. This valuable training aid — available at most bike shops or sporting-goods stores — holds your rear wheel upright and stationary, allowing you to pedal at a particular resistance or rpm. Pedal for 10 minutes for each leg, extending your resting leg to the side.

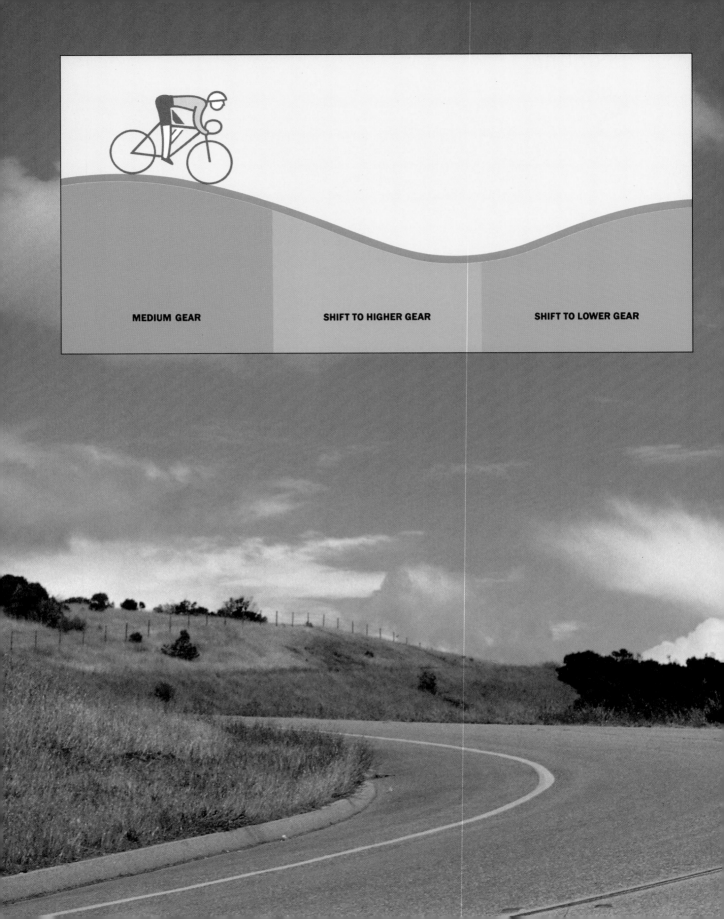

MEDIUM GEAR

SHIFT TO HIGHER GEAR

SHIFT TO LOWER GEAR

Gearing

Gearing is a necessary element of efficient pedaling, since it allows you to maintain a constant cadence over variable terrain. Efficient gearing depends on the incline and condition of the road. Adjust your gears whenever your cadence drops or increases for more than a few pedal rotations. If it drops, downshift to a lower gear; conversely, if it increases, shift into a higher gear.

Usually, you will need to adjust your gears only for hills. Proper gearing requires anticipation, as demonstrated in the illustration at left. You should shift gears as soon as you lose forward momentum; it might be necessary to shift several times in the course of an uphill run. When pedaling downhill, you should generally shift into a higher gear before you start spinning the pedals. Downhill momentum will allow you to maintain your cadence part of the way up the next grade — usually for 15 to 50 feet.

When starting up a hill, be sure to downshift before your cadence drops precipitously. For the derailleur to function, the chainwheel must spin evenly. If you shift too late and exert too much pressure on the pedals, the derailleur might not respond. In that case, you will have to slow your cadence for a few pedal rotations to allow the gearing mechanism to click in properly.

In standard derailleur systems, moving the shift levers changes gears by skipping the chain from one cog and chainwheel to another. Bicycle derailleur/chainring systems vary, so you will have to learn yours to know just how far the shift levers must be moved to change gears. Allow several seconds for the derailleur to make the shift. Index derailleur systems avoid some of the guesswork by clicking immediately into gear.

Braking

Effective braking is a vital bicycle-handling skill. However, proper braking technique is not only a safety factor, it also increases your riding efficiency by allowing you to decelerate appropriately as required.

Most of the stopping force comes from the front brake; while the rear brake does exert some braking power, its main function is balance. Get in the habit of applying both brakes simultaneously, since operating just the front brake could lock the front wheel and send you tumbling over the bike. Shifting your weight backward on the saddle will also help you to stop more quickly.

Braking on wet or slippery roads requires special attention, because the brake pads slip on the rims. It may take three times as long to stop in wet conditions, and you are at a greater risk of skidding. Anticipate slow-downs, and apply the brakes gently, allowing plenty of time to stop.

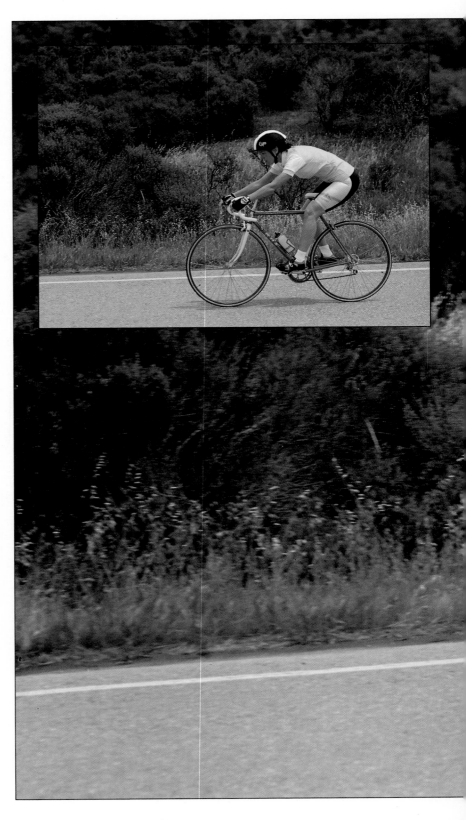

To slow or stop your bike gradually with your hands on the brake hoods, use your first two fingers of each hand to operate the levers *(right)*. **If you are slowing, apply greater pressure to the front brake than the rear, and shift your weight backward slightly. To be prepared to make an abrupt halt, you should practice the emergency stopping technique** *(inset)*. **Apply both brakes, putting more pressure on the front brake. Simultaneously slide your weight all the way back behind the saddle to increase the pressure on the rear wheel. Your arms should be straight.**

Riding a Line

Riding a straight line, and choosing a path around objects in the road as well as corners, sounds easier than it is. And following a line is an important skill that you must be able to maintain at all times. Not only does it make your movement predictable to cars and other riders, it also conserves energy otherwise wasted in unnecessary side-to-side adjustments.

Ideally you should follow a straight line about six inches from the shoulder of the road. Practice riding on a white line in an empty parking lot or a deserted stretch of road with no cars around. Then work on following the same line while you look over your shoulder.

Like most riding techniques, setting your line requires an awareness of the terrain and anticipation of what lies ahead. You want to veer from your line as little as possible: Plan ahead for maneuvers such as swerving around objects in your way or negotiating corners.

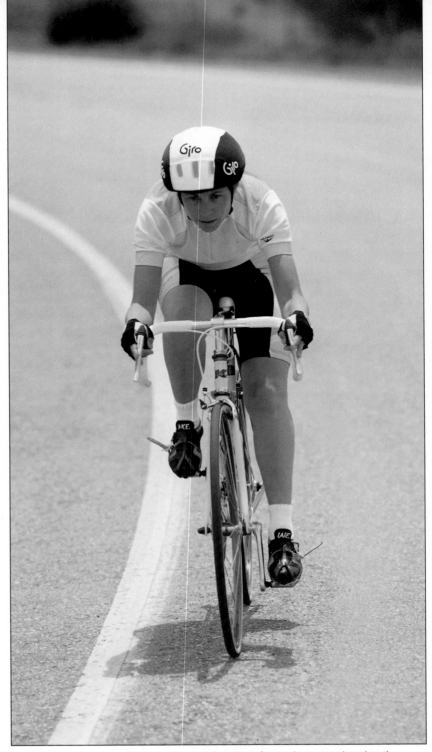

Riding a line is a function of two elements: choosing the correct focal point and body position. Experts recommend focusing about 20 feet ahead of you when riding 10 to 15 miles per hour; add one foot for each additional mile per hour. This distance allows you to see obstacles ahead and to make subtle adjustments. Your wrists and elbows should be relaxed as you grip the handlebars *(above)*.

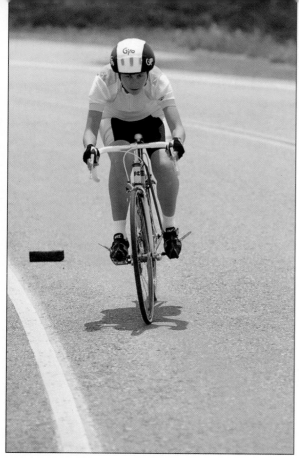

To avoid an obstacle in the road, use your hips to steer around it, leaning your body weight to the side as necessary. This will keep the front and rear tires in alignment and conserve your energy *(left)*. Relying on your focal point will allow you to anticipate the correct line to follow around an obstacle on the basis of the road and traffic conditions *(below)*.

Cornering

Successful cornering is accomplished by shifts in body weight. You should never steer with the handlebars while actually in a turn; rather, you should position the bike to follow a wide arc that will also allow you to coast through it. Prior to encountering the turn, flick your brakes to slow slightly, then lower your body and use a slight movement of your hips to lean in the direction of the turn *(left)*. Stop pedaling just before you enter the turn. Hold your pedals in the 12 o'clock/six o'clock position, with your weight completely on the outside pedal and your leg extended, and your inside knee bent *(above)*. You should be able to lean more than 30 degrees in a turn and still stay upright. Never brake abruptly while in a turn.

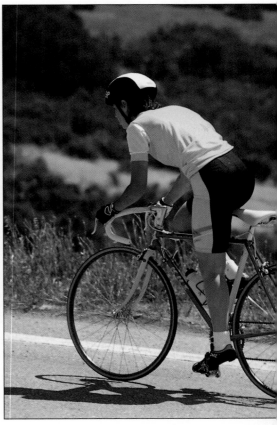

Hill Riding/1

Practice climbing short, gentle hills while seated *(above left).* **Place your hands midway on the handlebars, and slide backward slightly in the saddle to give you better leverage on the pedals. Use your arms to pull up slightly on the handlebars, rocking your upper body forward rhythmically to increase your momentum. It is easier to climb steeper hills while standing on the pedals** *(above right).* **With your hands widely spaced on the brake hoods, shift your body weight over the front of the bike.**

All your bicycle-handling skills come into play when tackling hills. Pedaling technique, gearing, braking, choosing a line and even cornering are included in successful hill navigation. Hill climbing also takes a considerable amount of upper-body strength, as pulling on the handlebars allows you to increase the force that you apply on the pedals.

Gear selection for both uphill and downhill riding should be based on staying as close as possible to your optimal cadence over level terrain. The correct gear to select depends on your fitness level, your climbing style and the grade and length of the hill. In general, if you climb while standing on the pedals, you will ride in a higher gear than if you climb in a seated position. However, it is essential that you anticipate gear shifts before you crank too hard at the pedals on the uphill, which makes it difficult to change gears, or spin the pedals too quickly on the downhill.

Avoid coasting after a long climb, even if you encounter a downhill immediately. It is better to keep your legs turning to avoid a build-up of lactic acid in your muscles.

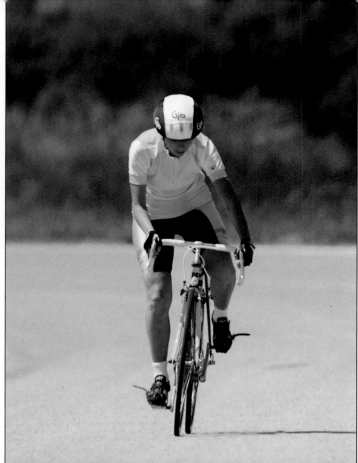

Leveraging is an effective way to utilize your upper-body strength when climbing from a standing position *(left)*. With your hands in a wide grip on the brake hoods, shift your body weight forward over the handlebars. As you perform each pedal downstroke, lean your body toward that leg to increase your pedaling force, alternating left and right *(below)*. This will create the sensation that you are throwing your bike back and forth. Your front and rear tires should stay in alignment.

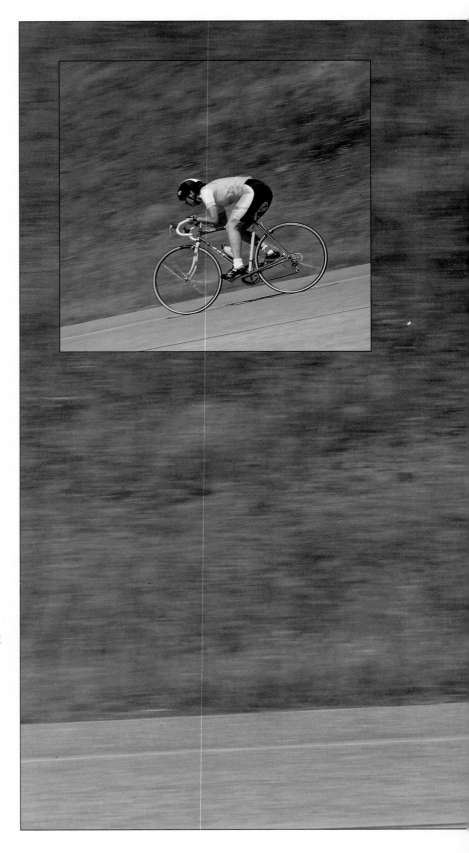

Hill Riding/2

Maximizing both speed and safety is the goal of skillful descents. The primary danger in downhill riding is losing control on a curve. Prepare for curves by keeping your hands on the brake hoods, ready to use the brakes to reduce speed before you enter the curve *(right)*. Raising your upper body to increase wind resistance will also help slow the bike. Remember not to brake while actually cornering, and to steer the bike by leaning. The tucked position *(inset)* optimizes speed on a downhill straightaway: Center your body weight over the back of the saddle, keep your knees close together, place your hands next to the stem, and lower your body and head as close to the top tube as possible. To increase your balance, place your pedals in the three o'clock/ nine o'clock position.

Group Riding

Group riding, called riding the paceline, or drafting, is more than social cycling. It is a time-honored training technique that allows riders to benefit by protecting one another from the effects of wind resistance.

A paceline is a closely packed formation of riders, one behind the other. The lead rider is said to be pulling the rest, as they benefit from the draft created behind him or her. Indeed, studies have shown that paceline riding can save 20 to 25 percent of a cyclist's energy. The paceline changes constantly, with a new rider assuming the lead position at a predetermined interval. Riding a paceline demands excellent bike-handling skills, since only a few inches separate you from the other riders.

When riding a single paceline, all cyclists should follow about 12 inches behind the wheel of the preceding rider. The lead rider's pull lasts between one and 10 minutes. He then eases off to one side, allowing his speed to slow so he falls back to position 1. As the last rider passes him, he starts to accelerate and swings back into line behind him at position 2. The formation rotates continually, as the other riders maintain speed, and the second rider assumes his pull at the front.

An echelon is a paceline that is adjusted diagonally to minimize the effects of a crosswind. In an echelon, the riders are angled downwind from the leader, with the front wheel of each bicycle approximately aligned with the rear wheel of the preceding bike.

The lead rider might pull for less than a minute. He then eases his pace, falling back to position 1 as he allows the second rider to pass him and assume the lead. After the last rider passes him, he accelerates and slips behind him into position 2.

2

FORWARD

1

WIND

All-Terrain Biking/1

The excitement and variety offered by all-terrain biking have made it the fastest-growing kind of cycling. Combining racing technology with the off-road capabilities of the popular children's BMX (bicycle motocross) stunt bikes, all-terrain bicycles — also called mountain bikes — can tackle steep, uneven trails. They have made accessible many areas formerly off-limits to the rider and, because of the special handling skills required, have presented new challenges even to experienced cyclists. Indeed, the added element of rough terrain makes good bike-handling skills even more crucial to safe and efficient riding.

Even though ATBs are ideally suited for rugged terrain, one of the more popular uses of off-road bicycles is for urban riding. The knobby tires that improve traction on uneven mountain trails do the same on potholed city roads. So, while its heavier frame means you will not be able to achieve the same on-road speeds with an ATB, it is perfectly appropriate as your only bicycle — unless you intend to get involved in road racing.

The off-road techniques on the following six pages demonstrate specific handling skills for mountain bikes and show how they vary from those of traditional racing.

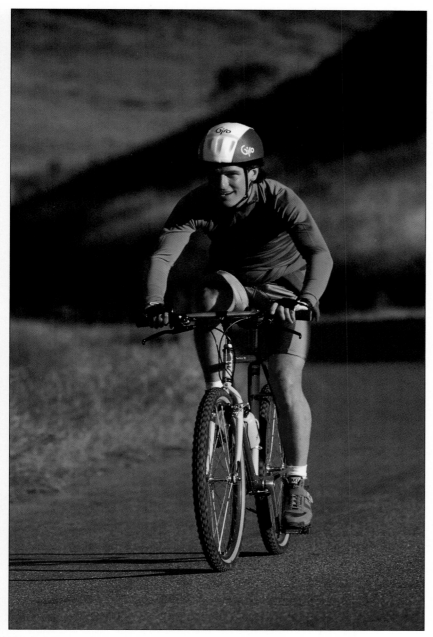

The upright posture is not as essential when riding your
ATB on a relatively smooth road, so bend your elbows to try
to lower yourself slightly into a more standard, aerodynamic
cycling position *(above)*.

A more upright posture and wider arm position *(left)* are the
primary variations between mountain and road bicycles. This
difference allows you to distribute your weight over a wider
area, thus increasing stability. When riding, focus on the path
ahead to prepare for upcoming rocks, roots or gullies.

All-Terrain Biking/2

Rising out of the saddle is usually the easiest way to go uphill on an ATB *(above)*. Bring your weight well forward over the handlebars, keeping your arms widely spaced to balance the front wheel.

Controlling the bike is significantly more difficult as the terrain becomes more pitted and uneven *(above)*. Use your upper-body strength to control the front wheel, while maintaining your pedaling momentum as long as possible. If pedaling slows so much as to become ineffective, walk your bike through the area to save your energy *(right)*. Stabilize the bike by holding it at both the handlebar and the saddle.

All-Terrain
Biking/3

Keep your weight as low as possible
when riding downhill on an ATB to
increase your stopping power. If you have
a quick-release saddle, lower it just as
you start down the hill. Shift your body
backward and plant your feet in the three
o'clock/nine o'clock position *(right)*. Flick
the brakes off and on, making sure not to
hold the front brake too long, since it can
lock the wheel. On steeper downhills
(inset), shift your weight to the rear of
the saddle, with your arms outstretched,
to stabilize the rear of the bike.

Strengtheners for Cyclists/1

Cycling is powered by the legs, particularly the quadriceps muscles in the front of the thigh. Strengthening exercises that work the hamstring muscles in the back of the thigh will help to balance this leg muscle development. This can make your cycling more effective, allowing you to push downward and pull upward on the pedals with equal force for proper pedaling action.

Strenuous uphill riding also makes substantial demands on the muscles of the upper body, so the strengthening program on these and the following four pages conditions the muscles of the shoulders and back, as well as those of the legs. Such exercises will enhance flexibility in these muscles, which often become stiff from long hours spent gripping the handlebars, while your torso is bent over on the saddle. A balanced strengthening program that allows you to relax the muscles of your upper body will permit you to ride more comfortably for a longer period of time.

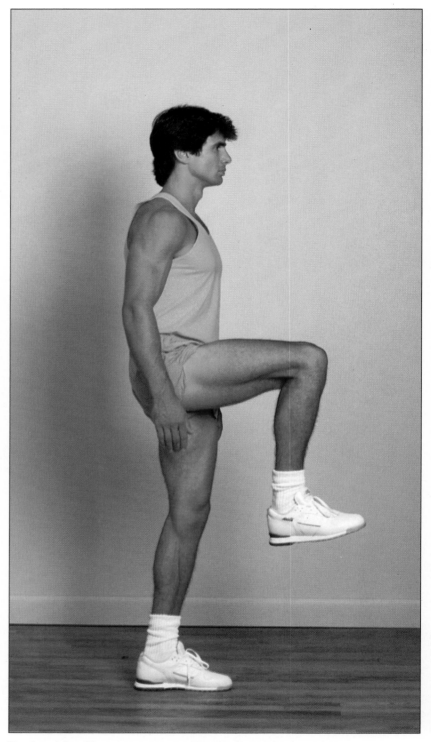

Stand straight with your arms at your sides. Bend your right knee and raise your leg to hip height, keeping your foot directly under your knee *(above)*; lower and alternate legs; repeat 10-20 times.

Lie prone with your hands on the floor in push-up position *(top)*. Perform a push-up, supporting your weight on your hands and feet *(above)*. Do not arch your back. Repeat 10-30 times.

Strengtheners
for Cyclists/2

Stand straight with your arms at your sides, about a foot and a half in front of a weight bench or low stool *(right)*. Simultaneously extend your arms in front of you and bend your knees. Keeping your lower back arched, continue lowering yourself into a squat. Stop just above the bench *(below)*; hold momentarily. Return to the starting position; repeat 10-20 times.

From a standing position *(above left)*, pick your left leg up high and lunge forward as far as possible, dropping your right knee almost to the ground *(above right)*. Thrust backward with your left leg and return to the starting position; switch legs; repeat 10-20 times.

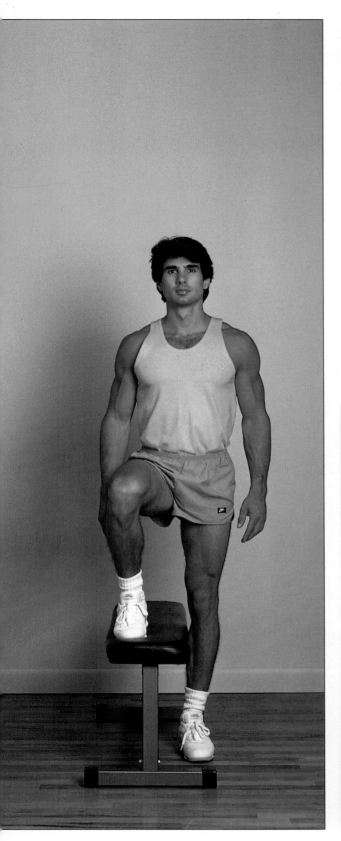

Stand next to a weight bench. Raise your left leg and rest your foot on the bench *(far left)*. Step up onto the bench with your right leg to a standing position *(center)*, then lower your left leg back to the floor on the other side of the bench *(left)*. Alternate this stepping motion with both legs 10-20 times.

Stand with your back against a wall, your feet hip-width apart and about two feet away from it, and your arms crossed in front of your chest. Bend your knees and slide downward so your thighs are parallel to the floor *(below)*. Hold for 20-60 seconds; return to the starting position; repeat two to three times.

CHAPTER FOUR

The Triathlon

Using competition to improve the quality of your training

Because it combines three endurance activities, the competitive event known as the triathlon is virtually synonymous with cross training. Indeed, the increasing use of cross training by athletes and fitness enthusiasts exemplifies the growth of this varied, demanding sport, which most often combines swimming, cycling and running. An estimated half-million triathletes, most of whom are amateurs, now compete each year in more than twelve hundred triathlons in the United States. In the most famous triathlon, the Ironman, competitors swim a grueling 2.4 miles in open water, then cycle 112 miles and finish with a 26.2-mile marathon — a feat that the top contenders accomplish in less than nine hours.

However, you do not need to possess the almost superhuman level of endurance required for the Ironman to be a triathlete, since most triathlons are considerably less demanding. A more typical triathlon consists of approximately a one-mile swim, a 25-mile cycling leg and a six-mile run. These distances, known collectively as the Short Course, are considered standard for each activity internationally. And healthy individuals in reasonably good shape can train for a Short Course triathlon in about two months.

Successful triathletes attain their competitive goals by improving the quality of their workouts rather than increasing the quantity of them. A landmark study at Ball State University's human performance laboratory suggests that most triathletes would benefit from more interval training — short, intense workouts interspersed with rest periods — and fewer long swims, rides and runs. In the study, 11 triathletes were measured for body fat level, percentage of slow- and fast-twitch muscle fibers and for oxygen uptake in all three events. While most of the subjects were found to be strong and well trained aerobically, the major performance obstacle they faced was lack of technical skill. The researchers advised that once you have established a solid foundation of muscular and cardiovascular endurance in each sport, you should begin to incorporate speed work and increase your attention to technique.

The nine-week program for a Short Course triathlon, on pages 108-113, maximizes the quality of your workouts. You are ready to undertake this program if you have had at least three to six months of endurance, or distance, conditioning in each sport. At that point, you should begin a training regimen that includes both longer, anaerobic-threshold workouts and short, sprinting sets to increase your aerobic capacity and boost your fast-twitch fiber development for bursts of speed. You can tailor the program to your individual needs by adding more sprint training or anaerobic threshold training for a specific event, by varying rest periods between intervals, or even by going back to an easier level if you feel you are overtraining.

Improving the quality of your workouts depends not only on developing your speed and endurance through interval training, but on enhancing your skill — your efficiency — in the three events. How much time you spend on technique should be based on your individual experience. For example, swimming usually consumes less time than the other two events in a triathlon, so swimming success is as dependent on technique as it is on endurance conditioning. Thus, your swimming program will benefit most if you include drills, such as those in Chapter Two, that enhance stroke efficiency. Also, since most triathlon swims occur in open water, which requires coping with cold-water currents, try to practice in open water before you compete. Since one difficulty that open-water swimming presents is orienting yourself, it is a good idea to become familiar with marker buoys and landmarks of the actual course. (See pages 116-117.)

The cycling and running segments of a triathlon can be more demanding than the swimming event because the swim occurs first, when you are strongest, and both cycling and running require greater amounts of time to complete. The skills required for the cycling leg, such as ascending and descending hills while riding in a group, come from practice rides and races. However, drafting, a group-riding

Choosing a Race

The lengths, locations, dates and relative difficulty of triathlons vary greatly throughout the United States. Choosing which race or races to enter, and knowing when you are sufficiently trained to compete with confidence, can be difficult. Here are some guidelines:

◆ **Are you ready?** If you can swim .6 miles in 31 minutes or less, cycle 7.5 miles in no more than 34 minutes, and run three miles in no more than 35 minutes — all within a period of five days — you will be comfortable competing in the standard United States Triathlon Series event of a one-mile swim, a 25-mile cycle and a six-mile run.

◆ **Which race should you enter?** The lengths of races vary from the so-called Tiny Tri of a .31-mile swim, a 12.4-mile cycle and a 3.1-mile run, which is tailored especially for beginners, to the six-day Ultraman event of a six-mile ocean swim, a 250-mile cycle (in two days) and a 52.4-mile run. Also consider how far you must travel. You will have to transport your bicycle as well as yourself, and you should spend the night before the event near the course, so that you will be well rested.

◆ **When should you enter?** Lists of upcoming triathlons and biathlons (or two-sport competitions, usually of biking and running) in your region are available from local triathlon clubs, as well as national lists published in magazines devoted to triathlon events.

technique demonstrated on pages 90-91 — a common energy-saving practice used in bike races — is not allowed in the triathlon.

Running is the final event of most triathlons, and many experts claim that it is the deciding factor, since, if you are not at your absolute best during the swimming or cycling legs, you have a chance to make up lost time in the run. For this reason, the quality of your running workouts is of vital importance. It is not necessary to run an inordinate amount of mileage, especially since more injuries occur in training for this event than for any other. Rather, routines that allow you to boost your anaerobic threshold are invaluable.

The comprehensive muscle development of triathletes may lead to decreases in flexibility, requiring some special performance techniques in each sport. For example, since endurance runners tend to have less flexibile ankles than competitive swimmers, a triathlete might benefit from using a shallow kick. Or, because runners tend to have less developed quadriceps than cyclists, a triathlete should utilize his or her hamstrings to get more pedaling power by positioning the saddle so that the downstroke leg is extended fully. The following pages will take you through the three sports of the triathlon and show you how to modify your technique to accommodate the muscle development caused by the endurance emphasis of cross training. They also demonstrate how to enhance your performance through drills, stretches and practicing transitions.

Nine-Week Triathlon Training Program

S *Swim*   **C** *Cycle*   **R** *Run*

All times are in minutes; workouts not designated AT or ST are distance workouts.

Optimizing your cross training regimen demands careful planning to ensure that you exercise all your muscles in a balanced way. Contrary to popular belief, this is not done by logging countless miles, which only increases the opportunity for injuries. Rather, elite triathletes emphasize the quality of workouts by including shorter, more intense sessions of anaerobic threshold and sprint training.

The nine-week training program presented here was designed by premier triathlete Dave Scott, six-time winner of Hawaii's famed Ironman Triathlon. It will prepare you for an international-distance triathlon of a one-mile swim, 25-mile bike ride and six-mile run. Before embarking on the program, you should have a basic level of aerobic fitness, with enough proficiency in each activity to be able to perform at least 20 consecutive minutes each of swimming, bicycling and running.

You should work out six days each week on the program, with two or three workout sessions on each day. Plan on investing about seven hours a week to your training to begin with; by the final week, you should have increased this amount to 12 hours a week. The workout times indicated include between three to eight minutes of warm-ups and three to five minutes of cool-downs; use the longer warm-up time for the first event of the day, and the longer cool-down for the last segment.

Starting with Week 2, include a set for anaerobic threshold (AT) training to each event once a week. In Week 3, add a set of sprint training (ST) to each activity per week. The structuring of these shorter, more intense sessions is detailed on pages 110-113. Workouts not designated as AT or ST sessions should be performed as distance training at 60 to 85 percent of your VO₂max time trial pace (refer to the pace charts on pages 20-21).

You can reorder your swim, cycle and run workouts and spread them throughout the day as your schedule permits. However, starting in Week 3, you should simulate a mini-triathlon on Saturdays: Perform each event in triathlon sequence, complete with transitions. Allow yourself five-minute transitions to start, and reduce this time as the weeks progress.

1

	Su	M	Tu	W	Th	F	Sa
	S-30	S-30	S-30			S-40	S-20
	C-35	C-35	C-25	C-35			C-35
	R-15	R-15		R-30	O	R-30	R-20

4

	Su	M	Tu	W	Th	F	Sa
	S-30 AT	S-35 ST	S-40 AT			S-40	S-30
	C-40 AT	C-45	C-35	C-50 ST			C-50
	R-25	R-20		R-35	O	R-35 ST	R-30

7

	Su	M	Tu	W	Th	F	Sa
	S-40 AT	S-45 ST	S-45	S-35		S-45	S-40
	C-55 AT	C-60	C-40	C-70 ST		C-50 ST	C-60
	R-35	R-30 ST		R-40 AT	O		R-45

AT *Anaerobic Threshold Training*   **ST** *Sprint Training*

2

Su	M	Tu	W	Th	F	Sa
S-30	S-30	S-30			S-40 AT	S-20
C-35 AT	C-35	C-25	C-35			C-35
R-15	R-15		R-30 AT	O	R-30	R-20

3

Su	M	Tu	W	Th	F	Sa
S-30 AT	S-35 ST	S-40 AT			S-40	S-30
C-40 AT	C-45	C-35	C-45 ST			C-45
R-25	R-20		R-35	O	R-35 ST	R-25

5

Su	M	Tu	W	Th	F	Sa
S-40 AT	S-40 ST	S-40	S-20		S-40	S-35
C-50 AT	C-55	C-35	C-60 ST			C-55
R-30	R-25		R-40 AT	O	R-45 ST	R-35

6

Su	M	Tu	W	Th	F	Sa
S-40 AT	S-40 ST	S-40	S-20		S-40	S-35
C-50 AT	C-55	C-35	C-65 ST			C-60
R-30	R-25		R-40 AT	O	R-45 ST	R-40

8

Su	M	Tu	W	Th	F	Sa
S-40 AT	S-45 ST	S-45	S-35		S-45	S-40
C-55 AT	C-60	C-40	C-70 ST		C-50 ST	C-70
R-35	R-30 ST		R-40 AT	O		R-50

9

Su	M	Tu	W	Th	F	Sa
S-30 AT	S-35 ST	S-40 AT			S-20	RACE DAY
C-40 AT	C-45	C-35	C-45 ST		C-20	RACE DAY
R-25	R-20 ST		R-35	O	R-15	RACE DAY

Anaerobic Threshold Training

For your anaerobic threshold training pace range, see page 21.

	SWIM	CYCLE	RUN
Interval duration	1.5-3 min.	1.5-3 min.	1.5-3 min.
Interval distance	50-300 yd.	¼-1½ mi.	300-800 yd.
Number of repeats	8-30	8-30	8-30
Rest interval	10-45 sec.	15 sec.-1 min.	15 sec.-1 min.
Training frequency	Once or twice per week	Once or twice per week	Once or twice per week
Sample workouts for each event	20 x 50 yd.	8 x ¾ mi.	8 x 440 yd.
	4 x 300 yd. 3 x 200 yd. 2 x 100 yd.	3 x ½ mi. 1 x 1 mi. 3 x ½ mi. 1 x 1 mi. 3 x ½ mi. 1 x 1 mi.	1 x 200 yd. 1 x 300 yd. 1 x 400 yd. 2 x 500 yd. 1 x 400 yd. 1 x 300 yd. 1 x 200 yd.

Anaerobic Threshold Training

Your anaerobic threshold is the point at which lactic acid is being synthesized faster than your muscles can diffuse it into your bloodstream. This causes you to feel intense fatigue, so you will only be able to sustain exercise at a level beyond your anaerobic threshold for a short time. Through training, you can boost this threshold so that you are able to push yourself further and faster without crossing it. This is done through interval work that trains your fast-twitch fibers to function more efficiently, thus delaying the build-up of lactic acid.

Perform a series of short intervals of 1.5 to three minutes at 75 to 90 percent of your VO_2max. Check the pace charts on pages 20-21 to determine your appropriate pace range based on your time trial. How long to rest between intervals varies from person to person; the time you will need is determined by your genetically determined distribution of fast- and slow-twitch fibers. If you have more fast-twitch fibers, you will require less rest between intervals than if your slow-twitch fibers predominate. Thus, determine the rest period between intervals by how you feel. Generally, you should allow your heart rate to drop only 10 to 15 percent between repeats. If your muscles burn and feel heavy, though, you should probably increase the rest interval.

Use the guidelines at left to structure your AT sessions in a variety of ways, as the sample workout sets illustrate. However, the actual intervals in each AT session should total at least 15 minutes.

Sprint Training

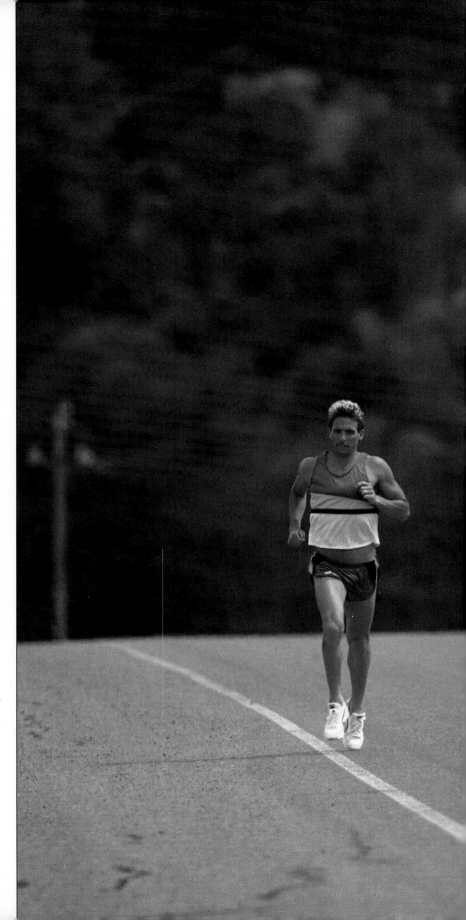

Sprinting will improve your performance times, since it enables you to function with oxygen debt and to endure lactic acid build-up. Sprint training requires that you perform very short intervals at all-out, 100-percent effort at speeds that exceed your VO₂max time trial pace.

You can sustain these speeds because the intervals are so brief — from 10 seconds to two minutes and covering minimum distances. However, because they entail such an intense effort, your rest time between sprints should be three times the length of the actual sprint (*see chart at right*). During the rest period, keep moving at a very slow speed. This is called active rest; it helps to minimize lactic acid build-up.

Use the pace chart for sprint training on pages 20-21 to determine your appropriate interval training pace, based on your time trial. Then use the guidelines at right to design your own sprint training workouts for each activity. Start at a low number of repeats — four per workout — and increase the amount as your body adapts to this training. You can measure the interval lengths by either distance or time, as shown in the sample workouts. Vary the composition of your intervals: For example, you may repeat the same distance, such as four 100-yard intervals, making sure to rest between each one for three times as long as it takes to perform. Or you may decrease the distances covered in your workouts periodically, and ladder your intervals, which involves increasing and then decreasing the distances again.

Sprint Training
For your sprint training pace range, see page 21.

	SWIM	CYCLE	RUN
Interval duration	10 sec.-2 min.	10 sec.-2 min.	10 sec.-2 min.
Interval distance	15-125 yd.	100 yd.-1 mi.	80-440 yd.
Number of repeats	4-8	4-8	4-8
Work/rest ratio	1:3	1:3	1:3
Training frequency	Once or twice per week	Once or twice per week	Once per week
Sample workouts for each event	4 x 100 yd.	4 x ½ mi.	6 x 80 yd.
	3 x 75 yd. 2 x 50 yd. 1 x 25 yd.	2 x ¼ mi. 1 x ½ mi. 2 x ¼ mi. 2 x ⅛ mi.	2 x 440 yd. 2 x 330 yd. 2 x 110 yd.

To compensate for tight shoulders, perform a slower, more powerful catch, with your wrist flexed and bent outward about 20-30 degrees *(above)*.

Maximize propulsion at the finish by hyperextending your wrist so your palm faces directly backward *(below)*.

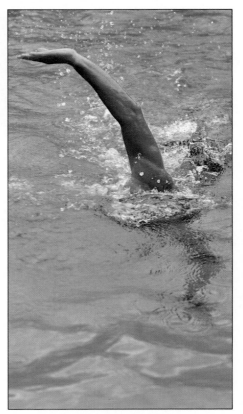

If you have tight arms and shoulders *(above)*, a wide recovery, with your hand higher than your elbow, will help to relax your shoulders.

Swimming

While swimming is almost always the lead-off event in a triathlon, it is usually the shortest leg of the race. Because it comprises a smaller percentage of your total triathlon effort, most triathletes do not perform an all-out swim.

The physiology of swimming makes it less demanding than either of the other two sports aerobically: Being horizontal in the water allows your cardiovascular system to pump as much as 20 percent more blood to your muscles than when you are in a vertical position. To maximize your training, work on improving stroke mechanics, using the techniques shown in Chapter Two as a guide, and conserve your leg strength.

The muscle development that results from cross training can alter stroke mechanics slightly, requiring some adjustments to maintain good form. For example, because they keep their arms forward while cycling, triathletes generally have less flexiblity in their shoulders than other swimmers do, resulting in a wider catch and higher arm recovery. Methods for dealing with such differences are shown on these two pages; preparing to swim in open water appears on pages 116-117.

Kicking should contribute only a little to your forward propulsion; save energy by keeping your kick shallow. Turning your toes inward slightly will increase your kicking efficiency and power *(below)*.

Practice sighting when swimming in a pool. Pick a landmark in front of you at the pool's edge, and raise your head straight out of the water to look forward at it every five strokes *(above)*.

Occasional bilateral breathing — breathing to both sides — will help keep you on course when swimming in open water, and will also alleviate shoulder discomfort *(right)*.

Open-Water Swimming

For many triathletes, swimming in an ocean or a lake presents the greatest challenge of the race. Open-water swimming is vastly different from pool swimming: The water is colder generally and there may be waves or currents; there are no lane markers for guidance. In addition, you might have to contend with the flailing arms and legs of other competitors.

Training for triathlon swimming requires some open-water sessions to get you acclimated to the colder temperature and familiar with laneless navigation. Start with short, 15-minute workouts, and increase the time gradually. Be sure to wear a swim cap, which will greatly reduce heat loss.

At the start of the race, maneuver through surf by diving beneath waves just before they break over you. Try not to be intimidated by the congestion at the start; at worst, you will sustain a kick, but it will be cushioned by the water. As the crowd thins, take advantage of other swimmers' forward propulsion by drafting, which is allowed in this event, and can save up to 20 percent of your energy: Follow slightly behind a swimmer going as fast or a little faster than you.

Sighting — keeping track of landmarks and buoys — keeps you on course as you navigate through open water. This can be espeically difficult when you are moving fast. A sighting drill is shown above.

Cycling

A majority of triathletes say that cycling is their weakest area. As in the other events, to accommodate the comprehensive muscle development of cross trainers as well as to conserve leg strength for running, you might need to make some specific adjustments in your cycling technique.

In particular, triathletes have well-developed hamstrings from running. To take advantage of this, you should emphasize your downstroke pedaling, rather than striving for the more balanced pedaling that other cyclists favor, which relies mainly on the quadriceps for the upstroke. You should also work at a cadence of about 80-95 rpms, which places more emphasis on your slow-twitch endurance fibers. On hills, reduce your cadence even further, to 60 rpms, or experiment with standing and using a higher gear.

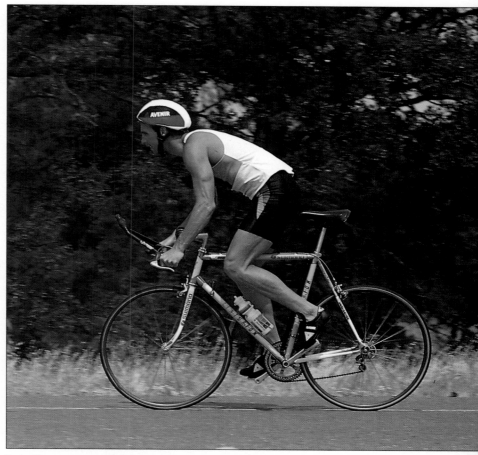

To build up your quadriceps for cycling — and enhance your anaerobic training — shift into high gear and pedal while standing. Perform four to eight repetitions for 20-60 seconds.

Aerodynamic handlebars *(left)* streamline your body posture, and have been shown to shave over a minute off every 25 miles. Varying your hand position on the handlebars frequently relaxes your triceps, deltoids and lower back; similarly, standing on the pedals stretches your lower back *(inset, far left)*. To accommodate differing patterns of muscle development, optimal sizing of your bike for a triathlon is slightly different from sizing for regular cycling. The saddle should be raised higher so your leg can be fully extended at the six o'clock position *(inset, left)* to allow for a more powerful downstroke.

Running

Triathletes tend to be strong runners. However, running is the last leg of the race, so your technique will be hampered by muscles that have tightened in the swimming and cycling events. On the other hand, strengthening your upper body through swimming will allow you to use your upper body muscles to help power you through the early part of the run.

When shifting from biking to running, you also have to contend with tight shoulder and back muscles from the bent-over cycling posture, and tight hip flexors from the continual hip rotation of pedaling. Concentrate on your respiration, taking slow, deep breaths, to help ease you into the run. Start with a shortened stride to accommodate tight hip flexors and allow your hamstrings to adjust to the workload. Increase your stride gradually as your muscles become more flexible. Do not lift your legs too high, since this places more stress on your hamstrings and hip flexors, also causing you to land harder, which increases the pounding absorbed by your feet and knees. Instead, increase the rate of your stride, rather than your stride length for the first half mile or mile, then return to your earlier rate.

To align your body correctly for triathlon running, shift your weight by leaning your upper body forward about five degrees *(above)*. Lower your head slightly, and focus your eyes 40-50 feet ahead.

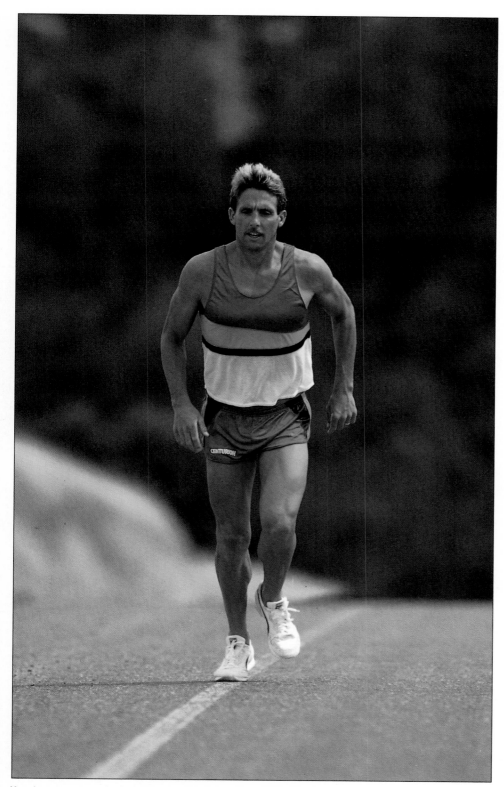

Keeping your upper body, including your face, relaxed will help you run more smoothly. Every half mile, drop your shoulders and shake your arms and fingers to facilitate relaxation *(above)*.

Transitions

Experienced triathletes know the value of smooth transitions: The amount of time you spend shifting from one leg of a triathlon to the next can decide the race. Becoming proficient at transitions requires practice; include them in your training program.

Effective transitions actually begin before the race, at your assigned transition location. Here, well in advance of the starting gun, you should organize the clothing and gear required for the race. Plan this layout so that the changes you will need to make during the race are minimal. For example, wear your swimsuit for the entire race, if possible. Many triathletes do not wear socks to save the time it takes to put them on.

Transitions include the actual physiological preparations for changing activities as well. Thus, use the minutes immediately preceding and following transitions for warm-up and cool-down stretches.

Have your transition gear laid out in a well-planned fashion *(above)*. Arrange your gear according to use: In front, have a towel for drying your feet. Behind this, place your shoes — ready to be tied (and socks, if you wear them) — and a rolled-up singlet. Your bike should be in back. Position your helmet on the handlebars or at the front wheel, with your gloves and sunglasses inside it.

If you have a clip-on shoe/pedal system, you can save time in the swim-to-bike transition by putting your shoes on while you begin riding *(right)*. Rub the inside rim of the shoes with petroleum jelly to make them slip on easily.

Anticipate transitions by doing some preliminary stretches in the moments before you finish an event. In the final stages of the cycling segment, stretch your back and hip flexors by placing your hands on the brake hoods and lowering yourself off the saddle, pushing your hips toward the stem. Drop one heel all the way downward, hold momentarily, then switch heel positions. Look up slightly and arch your back *(below)*.

CHAPTER FIVE

Eating for Performance

*The facts about
carbohydrate loading*

If you are serious about your endurance training, what should you eat to maximize your performance? Almost twenty years ago a team of Swedish researchers rigorously addressed this question by developing a dietary program to help endurance athletes increase their exercise time before becoming exhausted. The key to their program was to manipulate an athlete's intake of carbohydrate, a nutrient that is very important for fueling muscular endurance. The human body converts carbohydrates in food into blood sugar and glycogen, a form of carbohydrate that is stored in the muscles and the liver. When the supply of muscle glycogen is depleted, muscle fibers can no longer contract efficiently and fatigue occurs. Therefore, a diet that could either postpone glycogen depletion or increase the muscles' ability to store glycogen would be a boon to endurance athletes.

Carbohydrate loading, as the Swedish regimen came to be known, involved a two-step process: depletion and loading. One week before a competitive event, the athlete would first deplete his glycogen stores by exercising to exhaustion for three days while consuming a low-carbohydrate diet. Three or four days before competition, the athlete would reduce his exercise workload significantly and switch to a high-carbohydrate diet; the glycogen-starved muscles would then compensate for their depleted state by absorbing glycogen to the point of supersaturation. In studies conducted by the Swedish researchers, subjects stored two to three times the normal amount of muscle glycogen and increased the length of time they could exercise.

Many athletes have found, however, that this classic method of carbohydrate loading is not always the most beneficial: Not only does this regimen disrupt normal training and diet patterns, but forced depletion of carbohydrates does not appear to enhance a trained muscle's ability to replenish glycogen. Well-trained athletes naturally deplete their muscle glycogen in the course of their day-to-day exercise programs. As an adaptation to training, their muscle fibers increase their capacity for storing glycogen if adequate carbohydrates are in the diet. Moreover, sharply depleting the body's glycogen level has caused physiological side effects such as dizziness, soreness and fatigue; the subsequent loading phase may be accompanied by water retention so that an athlete feels bloated and stiff. For these reasons, a growing number of nutritionists and sports medicine specialists have advised that the depletion and deprivation phases of carbohydrate loading should be avoided.

Most experts, in fact, now recommend that you forgo any phase of a diet that emphasizes low levels of carbohydrates. You can prepare yourself for even the heaviest training programs by eating what is now considered to be a well-balanced diet. As the guidelines on the opposite page indicate, you should obtain about 55 to 65 percent of your calories from carbohydrates, preferably complex ones such as vegetables, legumes, breads, cereals and pastas.

To prepare for a competition, you can begin an extra-high carbohydrate diet three or four days prior to the actual event. This diet should contain your usual number of calories, but increase the percentage of carbohydrate calories to 70 to 80 percent. Use the recipes in this chapter, which all are within that range, to help plan your meals. Be sure to consume plenty of fluids during this carbohydrate-loading phase, as well as during the competition itself.

Eat your last big high-carbohydrate meal 14 to 16 hours before your event. Avoid very spicy, salty or high-fiber foods, which can upset your digestive system. At bedtime the night before you compete, have a high-carbohydrate snack, such as the Apple-Raisin Biscuits on page 129 or the Dosas on page 141. Then have an additional snack three to four hours prior to competition.

This modified regimen has been shown to work effectively. In several studies, athletes who followed a diet containing 70 percent of the calories from carbohydrates did not suffer from a low level of glycogen even after several successive days of prolonged, vigorous

The Basic Guidelines

For a moderately active adult, the National Institutes of Health recommends a diet that is low in fat, high in carbohydrates and moderate in protein. The institutes' guidelines suggest that no more than 30 percent of your calories come from fat, that 55 to 60 percent come from carbohydrates and that no more than 15 percent come from protein. A gram of fat equals nine calories, while a gram of protein or carbohydrate equals four calories; therefore, if you eat 2,100 calories a day, you should consume approximately 60 grams of fat, 315 grams of carbohydrate and no more than 75 grams of protein daily. If you follow a lowfat/high-carbohydrate diet, your chance of developing heart disease, cancer and other life-threatening diseases may be considerably reduced.

The nutrition charts that accompany each of the lowfat/high-carbohydrate recipes in this book include the number of calories per serving, the number of grams of fat, carbohydrate and protein in a serving, and the percentage of calories derived from each of these nutrients. In addition, the charts provide the amount of calcium, iron and sodium per serving.

Calcium deficiency may be associated with periodontal disease — which attacks the mouth's bones and tissues, including the gums — in both men and women, and with osteoporosis, or bone shrinking and weakening, in the elderly. The deficiency may also contribute to high blood pressure. The recommended daily allowance for calcium is 800 milligrams a day for men and women. Pregnant and lactating women are advised to consume 1,200 milligrams daily; a National Institutes of Health consensus panel recommends that postmenopausal women consume 1,200 to 1,500 milligrams of calcium daily.

Although one way you can reduce your fat intake is to cut your consumption of red meat, you should make sure that you get your necessary iron from other sources. The Food and Nutrition Board of the National Academy of Sciences suggests a minimum of 10 milligrams of iron per day for men and 18 milligrams for women between the ages of 11 and 50.

High sodium intake is associated with high blood pressure. Most adults should restrict sodium intake to between 2,000 and 2,500 milligrams a day, according to the National Academy of Sciences. One way to keep sodium consumption in check is not to add table salt to food.

exercise. In comparison, subjects who followed a diet in which only 40 to 50 percent of the calories came from carbohydrates had less available glycogen. Researchers have also found that loading up on carbohydrates following an endurance event is an effective way to rebuild glycogen reserves. One university study showed that athletes who ate carbohydrates within two hours of a strenuous exercise session stored more carbohydrates from the meal than subjects who waited a longer period.

Bear in mind, however, that carbohydrate loading will only benefit you for nonstop events or intense training sessions longer than 90 minutes. For middle-distance races, extra carbohydrates do not appear to offer any advantage. More important, carbohydrate loading cannot compensate for the lack of a sound diet or training; only well-trained muscles can put extra carbohydrates to use.

Five-Vegetable Hash Browns

Breakfast

FIVE-VEGETABLE HASH BROWNS

Carbohydrates fuel your body, but vitamins are also important for optimal health. This dish supplies more than 50 milligrams of vitamin C.

CALORIES per serving	250
73% Carbohydrate	47 g
7% Protein	5 g
20% Fat	6 g
CALCIUM	68 mg
IRON	2 mg
SODIUM	209 mg

1 pound new potatoes
1/2 pound carrots
1/2 pound parsnips
1/4 pound sweet potatoes
1/4 pound turnips
1 medium-size onion
2 ounces shallots

2 teaspoons margarine
1 tablespoon olive oil
2 teaspoons sugar
1/4 teaspoon salt
1/2 teaspoon black pepper
1/4 cup chopped fresh parsley

Wash and trim the new potatoes, carrots, parsnips, sweet potatoes and turnips, and cut them into 1/2-inch-thick slices. Bring 3/4 cup of water to a boil in a large nonstick skillet over medium-high heat. Add the vegetables, return the water to a boil and cover the skillet. Cook for 5 to 7 minutes, or until the vegetables are crisp-tender, opening the pan to stir the vegetables several times. Meanwhile, peel and thinly slice the onion and shallots.

Transfer the vegetables to a bowl and cover it loosely with foil. Wipe the skillet with paper towels. Melt the margarine in the skillet over medium heat, then add the onion and shallots, and sauté for 2 minutes, or until the onion is golden. Drain and discard any liquid from the bowl and return the vegetables to the skillet, then add the oil, sugar and salt. Cook the vegetables, stirring frequently from the bottom of the pan, for 10 to 15 minutes, or until tender and browned. Add pepper to taste and sprinkle the vegetables with parsley. Divide the vegetables among 4 plates, and serve. Makes 4 servings

WHOLE-WHEAT QUICK BREAD

A thick slice of bread is a good foundation for breakfast. Top it with a fruit spread or part skim-milk ricotta or mozzarella cheese.

Vegetable cooking spray
1 1/2 cups whole-wheat flour
1/2 cup unbleached
   all-purpose flour, approximately
1 teaspoon baking powder
3/4 teaspoon baking soda

Pinch of salt
1 egg, lightly beaten
1 cup buttermilk
1/3 cup honey
1 tablespoon margarine, melted
   and cooled

CALORIES per serving	182
74% Carbohydrate	35 g
12% Protein	6 g
14% Fat	3 g
CALCIUM	77 mg
IRON	1 mg
SODIUM	206 mg

Preheat the oven to 350° F. Spray an 8-inch round baking pan with cooking spray and dust it with all-purpose flour. In a medium-size bowl stir together the whole-wheat flour, 1/2 cup of all-purpose flour, the baking powder, baking soda and salt, and make a well in the center. Add the buttermilk, honey and margarine to the egg, then add the egg mixture to the dry ingredients and stir just until combined. Turn the batter into the pan and bake for 35 minutes, or until a toothpick inserted in the center of the bread comes out clean and dry. Turn the bread out onto a rack to cool before serving. Makes 8 servings

APPLE-RAISIN BISCUITS

A pre-workout breakfast of fruit-filled biscuits offers plenty of carbohydrates to ensure a ready supply of energy for exercise.

2 cups unbleached all-purpose
   flour, approximately
2 tablespoons brown sugar
2 teaspoons baking powder
1/2 teaspoon ground cinnamon
Pinch of salt

3 tablespoons margarine,
   well chilled
3/4 cup skim milk
1 cup dried apples,
   coarsely chopped
1/3 cup golden raisins

CALORIES per biscuit	87
73% Carbohydrate	16 g
8% Protein	2 g
19% Fat	2 g
CALCIUM	39 mg
IRON	1 mg
SODIUM	79 mg

Preheat the oven to 425° F. In a medium-size bowl stir together 2 cups of flour, the sugar, baking powder, cinnamon and salt. Using a pastry blender or 2 knives, cut in the margarine until the mixture resembles coarse crumbs. Stir in the milk, then add the apples and raisins, and stir just until combined. Form the dough into a ball on a lightly floured work surface and, using a lightly floured rolling pin, roll it out to a 9-inch circle about 1/2 inch thick. Using a 2-inch biscuit cutter, cut 20 biscuits. Place them on a nonstick baking sheet and bake for 10 minutes, or until golden brown on top. Makes 20 biscuits

Lunch

OATMEAL BREAD

Oatmeal is a whole grain, so it retains its bran layer. Oat bran is particularly beneficial; it is rich in soluble fiber, which has been shown to reduce blood cholesterol. Aerobic exercise may also help lower cholesterol levels.

2 cups whole-wheat flour	Pinch of salt
2 1/2 cups unbleached all-purpose flour, approximately	1 cup skim milk
	2 tablespoons brown sugar
1 1/4 cups rolled oats	1 egg
1 package quick-acting dry yeast	Vegetable cooking spray

In a medium-size bowl stir together the whole-wheat flour, 1 1/2 cups of all-purpose flour, 1 cup of oats, the yeast and salt, and make a well in the center; set aside. Combine the milk, sugar and 1 cup of water in a small saucepan over low heat and bring it to 110° F (just warm to the touch). Meanwhile, separate the egg; place the white in a small bowl, cover with plastic wrap and set aside. Beat the yolk in a small bowl, then beat in 1/4 cup of the milk mixture. Add both milk mixtures to the dry ingredients, and stir until a dough forms. Turn the dough onto a lightly floured board and knead it for 5 to 7 minutes, kneading in the remaining all-purpose flour as needed. Place the

Oatmeal Bread

CALORIES per serving	164
78% Carbohydrate	32 g
15% Protein	6 g
7% Fat	1 g
CALCIUM	35 mg
IRON	2 mg
SODIUM	22 mg

dough in a medium-size bowl, cover it with a damp kitchen towel and set aside in a warm place to rise for 45 minutes, or until doubled in bulk.

Preheat the oven to 400° F. Spray a baking sheet with cooking spray. Punch the dough down and knead it on a lightly floured board for 1 to 2 minutes. Form the dough into an 8-inch round and place it on the baking sheet; set aside, uncovered, for 15 minutes. Beat the egg white and spread it generously over the top of the loaf with a pastry brush, then sprinkle the loaf with the remaining oats. Bake for 25 minutes, or until the bread is golden brown and sounds hollow when tapped on the bottom. Cool the bread on a rack before serving.

Makes 16 servings

CHUNKY FRUIT BUTTER

Unlike mayonnaise-dressed salads, this sandwich filling is low in fat. Natural sugars in the fruit provide abundant carbohydrates.

2 large Granny Smith apples	1/3 cup dark raisins
1/4 pound dried apricots	1/4 teaspoon ground ginger

Wash and core but do not peel the apples; cut them into large chunks. Bring 1 inch of water to a boil in a pan that will accommodate a vegetable steamer. Place the apples, apricots and raisins in the steamer, cover the pan and reduce the heat to medium-low so that the water simmers. Steam the fruit for 10 to 15 minutes, or until the apples are tender when pierced with the tip of a knife. Transfer the cooked fruit to a food processor or blender, add the ginger and process for 1 minute, or until blended but still chunky. (If you prefer a smoother butter, process until puréed.) Transfer the butter to a jar, cover and refrigerate it. The fruit butter will keep for up to 1 week.

Makes 10 servings (about 2 tablespoons each)

CALORIES per serving	62
94% Carbohydrate	16 g
4% Protein	1 g
2% Fat	.2 g
CALCIUM	10 mg
IRON	1 mg
SODIUM	2 mg

VEGETABLE PUREE SANDWICH

This sandwich is an outstanding source of vitamins A and C, and also contains a substantial amount of iron. Iron deficiency can hinder aerobic endurance by decreasing oxygen transport in the body's tissues.

1/2 pound carrots	2 tablespoons chopped fresh dill
1/2 pound turnips	1 medium-size cucumber
1/2 pound sweet potatoes	Eight 1/2-inch-thick slices
1 tablespoon Dijon mustard	Vegetable Bread (page 133)

Wash the carrots, turnips and potatoes. Trim the carrots, peel the turnips and potatoes, and cut the vegetables into large chunks. Bring 1 inch of water to a boil in a pan that will accommodate a large vegetable steamer. Place the vegetables in the steamer and cook, covered, for 10 minutes, or until tender when pierced with a sharp knife; set aside to cool.

Place the vegetables in a medium-size bowl and mash them until smooth. Add the mustard and dill, and stir until blended; set aside. Peel and slice the cucumber. Toast the bread and spread about 2/3 cup of the vegetable purée on each of 4 slices. Top the purée with cucumber slices and place a second slice of toast on each sandwich. Serve immediately.

Makes 4 servings

CALORIES per serving	407
77% Carbohydrate	80 g
12% Protein	12 g
11% Fat	5 g
CALCIUM	93 mg
IRON	4 mg
SODIUM	597 mg

RYE BREAD

CALORIES per serving	114
70% Carbohydrate	20 g
10% Protein	3 g
20% Fat	3 g
CALCIUM	14 mg
IRON	1 mg
SODIUM	96 mg

You should eat a high-carbohydrate meal within two hours after exercising in order to replenish your body's glycogen stores most efficiently. Fulfill your need for carbohydrates by planning your post-workout meal around a homemade bread like this one. The yeast in the bread adds biotin, a B vitamin that plays a role in glycogen synthesis.

1 1/2 cups light rye flour
1 cup whole-wheat flour
1 cup unbleached all-purpose flour, approximately
1/2 teaspoon salt
1 package dry yeast
2 tablespoons molasses

1 tablespoon cider vinegar
2 tablespoons malted grain beverage mix (instant coffee substitute)
3 tablespoons margarine, melted
2 teaspoons caraway seeds

In a medium-size bowl stir together the rye flour, whole-wheat flour, 1 cup of all-purpose flour and the salt, and make a well in the center; set aside. Place the yeast in a small bowl, add 1/4 cup of warm water (105-115° F) and set aside for 2 to 3 minutes. Meanwhile, in a small bowl stir together the molasses, vinegar, grain beverage and 3/4 cup of water. Pour the yeast mixture, the molasses mixture, the margarine and caraway seeds into the dry ingredients, and stir to form a dough. Turn the dough onto a lightly floured board and knead it for 5 to 7 minutes, or until smooth and elastic. Transfer the dough to a medium-size bowl, cover it with a damp kitchen towel and set aside in a warm place to rise for 1 hour, or until doubled in bulk.

Punch down the dough and knead it for 2 minutes on a lightly floured surface. Return the dough to the bowl, cover and let it rise for about 30 minutes, or until almost doubled in bulk.

Spray a 9 x 5-inch loaf pan with cooking spray and dust it lightly with flour. Punch down the dough again and roll it into a ball with your hands, then flatten it into an 8-inch disk. Roll up the dough to form a log. Place the dough in the pan and set it aside to rise, uncovered, for 30 minutes.

Preheat the oven to 450° F. Bake the bread for 10 minutes, then reduce the oven temperature to 325° F and bake for 35 minutes more, or until the loaf is golden brown and sounds hollow when tapped. Turn the bread out on a rack to cool for at least 10 minutes before serving.   Makes 16 servings

CALORIES per serving	116
73% Carbohydrate	22 g
17% Protein	5 g
10% Fat	1 g
CALCIUM	34 mg
IRON	2 mg
SODIUM	34 mg

CREAMY MUSHROOM BARLEY SOUP

This soup is a good source of niacin, a B vitamin that plays a part in the body's release of energy from carbohydrates.

1/2 pound onions
2 garlic cloves
2 cups low-sodium chicken stock
6 tablespoons barley

1/2 pound fresh mushrooms
1/4 cup chopped fresh parsley
2 tablespoons chopped fresh dill

Peel and coarsely chop the onions and garlic; set aside. Bring the stock and 2 cups of water to a boil in a medium-size saucepan over medium-high heat. Stir in the onions, garlic and barley, cover the pan, reduce the heat to low and simmer for 45 minutes. Meanwhile, wash, trim and coarsely chop the mushrooms; set aside.

Add the mushrooms to the soup, cover the pan and simmer for another 15 minutes. Using a slotted spoon, transfer the solids to a food processor or blender and process until puréed. Return the purée to the saucepan, then stir in the parsley and dill. Bring the soup to a boil over medium-high heat, then ladle it into 4 bowls and serve.   Makes 4 servings

VEGETABLE BREAD

Carrots are an excellent source of beta-carotene, which the body converts into vitamin A. Research has revealed vitamin A to be involved in glycogen synthesis and in the synthesis of muscle protein, two functions important in endurance and strength training.

CALORIES per serving	154
75% Carbohydrate	29 g
13% Protein	5 g
12% Fat	2 g
CALCIUM	23 mg
IRON	2 mg
SODIUM	161 mg

1 cup cooked kidney beans,
  or canned kidney beans, rinsed
  and well drained
2 cups grated carrots
1 1/2 cups finely chopped
  scallions
2 garlic cloves, minced
1 package dry yeast

3 cups unbleached
  all-purpose flour
1 1/4 cups whole-wheat
  flour, approximately
1 teaspoon salt
1/2 teaspoon ground pepper
2 tablespoons margarine
Vegetable cooking spray

Mash the beans in a medium-size bowl, then add the carrots, scallions and garlic, and stir until combined; set aside. Place the yeast in a small bowl, add 3/4 cup of warm water (105-115° F) and set aside for 2 to 3 minutes. Meanwhile, in a large bowl stir together the all-purpose flour, 1 cup of whole-wheat flour, the salt and pepper, and make a well in the center. Pour in the yeast mixture, the vegetables and the margarine, and stir until well combined; the mixture will form a fairly sticky dough. Flour the work surface with 2 tablespoons of whole-wheat flour. Knead the dough for 5 to 7 minutes, or until smooth and elastic, kneading in more flour if necessary. Transfer the dough to a medium-size bowl, cover it with a damp kitchen towel and set aside in a warm place to rise for 1 to 1 1/2 hours, or until doubled in bulk.

Punch down the dough. Sprinkle another 2 tablespoons of whole-wheat flour on the work surface and knead the dough for 2 minutes. Return the dough to the bowl, cover and let it rise for about 1 hour, or until almost doubled in bulk.

Spray a baking sheet with cooking spray. Punch down the dough again and knead it briefly on a lightly floured surface. Form the dough into a 7-inch round and place it on the baking sheet to rise, uncovered, for 30 minutes.

Preheat the oven to 425° F. Bake the bread for 10 minutes, then reduce the oven temperature to 325° F and bake for 45 to 50 minutes more, or until the loaf is golden brown and sounds hollow when tapped. Turn the bread out on a rack to cool for at least 10 minutes before serving.   Makes 16 servings

Dinner

POTATO PIZZAS

When not laden with fatty sausage, a heavy layer of high-fat cheese and lots of oil, pizza makes an ideal dinner. This vegetable-topped version is a good source of niacin and potassium, and it also supplies more than 4 grams of dietary fiber.

CALORIES per serving	402
72% Carbohydrate	72 g
11% Protein	11 g
17% Fat	8 g
CALCIUM	56 mg
IRON	4 mg
SODIUM	341 mg

1 package dry yeast
2 1/3 cups unbleached all-purpose flour, approximately
1 tablespoon margarine, melted
1/2 teaspoon salt, approximately
1/2 pound small red potatoes
4 firm-ripe plum tomatoes

1 medium-size red onion
1 tablespoon cornmeal
1 tablespoon olive oil
1 tablespoon grated Parmesan
1 teaspoon dried oregano
1/4 teaspoon ground pepper
1/4 cup chopped fresh parsley

Place the yeast in a large bowl and add 2/3 cup of warm water (105-115° F); stir to combine and set aside for 3 to 5 minutes. Add 1/3 cup of flour and stir until smooth, then add the margarine, 1/2 teaspoon of salt and the remaining flour, and stir until the mixture forms a cohesive dough. Transfer the dough to a lightly floured board and knead for 5 to 10 minutes, or until the dough is

Potato Pizzas

smooth and elastic. Place the dough in a medium-size bowl, cover it with a damp kitchen towel and set it aside in a warm place to rise for 1 hour, or until the dough is doubled in bulk. Meanwhile, wash the potatoes, place them in a small saucepan with cold water to cover and bring to a boil over medium-high heat. Reduce the heat to medium and simmer, uncovered, for 10 to 15 minutes, or until the potatoes are just tender when pierced with a sharp knife. Drain the potatoes and set them aside to cool.

When the dough has risen, punch it down and divide it into 4 pieces. Wrap each piece in plastic wrap and refrigerate until needed. Wash the tomatoes and peel the onion, then cut the tomatoes, onion and potatoes into 1/4-inch-thick slices; cover them loosely with plastic wrap and set aside.

Preheat the oven to 500° F. Dust the work surface and a rolling pin with cornmeal. Roll each portion of dough into a ball, flatten it into a disk, then roll it out to a 7-inch circle about 1/8 inch thick. Place the circles of dough on a nonstick baking sheet. Top each pizza crust with onions, then with potato and tomato slices. Drizzle olive oil over the pizzas, then sprinkle each one with Parmesan, oregano, pepper and a pinch of salt. Bake the pizzas for 10 minutes, then reduce the oven temperature to 400° F and bake for 5 to 7 minutes more, or until the crusts are golden. Sprinkle the pizzas with parsley, and serve immediately. Makes 4 servings

SPAGHETTI WITH TURKEY-TOMATO SAUCE

White meat turkey has the lowest fat content of any meat or poultry. Substituting turkey for ground beef or sausage in spaghetti sauce and adding lots of vegetables are two easy ways to make a healthier sauce.

CALORIES per serving	427
72% Carbohydrate	77 g
13% Protein	14 g
15% Fat	7 g
CALCIUM	90 mg
IRON	4 mg
SODIUM	268 mg

2 ounces ground turkey
1 tablespoon plus
   1 teaspoon chopped garlic
1 teaspoon dried oregano
1/4 teaspoon pepper
Pinch of salt
2 tablespoons olive oil
1 1/2 cups chopped onions

3/4 cup chopped celery
3/4 cup chopped carrots
1 bay leaf
Two 14-ounce cans plum tomatoes
1 tablespoon cornstarch
18 ounces spaghetti
1 tablespoon chopped
   fresh parsley

In a small bowl stir together the turkey, 1 teaspoon of garlic, 1/2 teaspoon of oregano, the pepper and salt. Cover loosely and set aside. For the sauce, heat the oil in a medium-size saucepan over medium heat, add the onions and the remaining garlic, and sauté for 5 minutes, or until the onions are translucent. Add the celery, carrots, bay leaf and remaining oregano. Reserving 1/2 cup of the liquid, add the tomatoes and the remaining liquid to the pan and bring to a boil over medium-high heat. Cover the pan, reduce the heat to low and simmer the sauce for 10 minutes. Meanwhile, stir together the cornstarch and reserved tomato liquid in a cup.

Increase the heat to medium-high, bring the sauce to a boil and stir in the cornstarch mixture. Add the turkey, breaking it up with a spoon. Reduce the heat to medium-low, partially cover the pan and simmer the sauce for 15 minutes more. Meanwhile, bring a large pot of water to a boil and cook the spaghetti for 10 to 12 minutes, or according to the package directions, until al dente. Drain the spaghetti and divide it among 6 plates. Top each serving with 3/4 cup of sauce, sprinkle with parsley and serve. Makes 6 servings

FETTUCCINE WITH VEGETABLES

Pasta is a good source of riboflavin, which aids in energy metabolism.

CALORIES per serving	497
72% Carbohydrate	90 g
18% Protein	23 g
10% Fat	6 g
CALCIUM	157 mg
IRON	4 mg
SODIUM	340 mg

1/2 pound green beans
1/2 pound yellow squash
1 cup lowfat cottage cheese (1%)
1/3 cup skim milk
2 tablespoons chopped
 fresh parsley
1 tablespoon margarine
1/2 pound red onions, sliced
2 garlic cloves, chopped
3/4 pound fettuccine
1 1/2 cups frozen corn kernels
1/2 teaspoon dried summer savory
 or basil
1/4 teaspoon white pepper
Pinch of salt
1 tablespoon grated Parmesan

Wash and trim the beans and squash. Cut the beans into 2-inch lengths. Halve the squash lengthwise and slice it 1/4 inch thick; set aside. Process the cottage cheese in a blender until smooth. With the machine running, add the milk, and process for 5 seconds. Stir in the parsley; set aside.

Bring a large pot of water to a boil. Meanwhile, melt the margarine in a medium-size skillet over medium heat. Add the onions and garlic, and cook, stirring, for 5 minutes. Cook the fettuccine for 8 to 10 minutes, or according to the package directions, until al dente. Meanwhile, add the beans, squash, corn, savory, pepper and salt to the skillet, and cook, stirring frequently, for 10 minutes, or until the vegetables are crisp-tender.

Drain the fettuccine and transfer it to a large serving bowl. Add the cheese sauce and vegetables, and toss to combine. Sprinkle the pasta and vegetables with Parmesan, and serve immediately.   Makes 4 servings

RATATOUILLE SOUP

Calcium and potassium, both vital to muscle function, are abundantly supplied by the vegetables in this soup.

CALORIES per serving	165
78% Carbohydrate	36 g
15% Protein	7 g
7% Fat	1 g
CALCIUM	212 mg
IRON	5 mg
SODIUM	42 mg

1/2 pound eggplant
6 ounces zucchini
1/4 pound carrots
1/4 pound onions
2 garlic cloves
Two 14-ounce cans
 low-sodium tomatoes
2 tablespoons chopped
 fresh parsley
1 teaspoon dried basil
1/2 teaspoon dried oregano
1/8 teaspoon ground pepper
Pinch of sugar
1 bay leaf

Wash, trim and dice the eggplant, zucchini and carrots. Peel and coarsely chop the onions and garlic; set aside. Place the tomatoes and their liquid in a medium-size saucepan and bring to a boil over medium-high heat. Add the eggplant, zucchini, carrots, onions, garlic, parsley, basil, oregano, pepper, sugar and bay leaf. Cover the pan, reduce the heat to medium-low and simmer the vegetables for 30 minutes.

Remove the pan from the heat, and allow the soup to cool slightly; remove and discard the bay leaf. Transfer 3 cups of the solids to a food processor or blender and process for 1 minute, or until coarsely puréed. Return the purée to the pan and stir to combine. Reheat the soup and serve it hot, or refrigerate it until well chilled and serve it cold.   Makes 2 servings

Biscotti

Desserts
········

BISCOTTI

The dried fruit in these cookies is a good source of magnesium.

3 cups unbleached
   all-purpose flour
1 teaspoon baking powder
Pinch of salt
5 tablespoons margarine
2/3 cup sugar

3 eggs
1 tablespoon grated lemon peel
1 tablespoon lemon juice
3/4 teaspoon anise extract
1 cup currants
3/4 cup chopped dried apricots

CALORIES per cookie	69
71% Carbohydrate	12 g
8% Protein	1 g
21% Fat	2 g
CALCIUM	12 mg
IRON	1 mg
SODIUM	31 mg

Preheat the oven to 350° F. In a medium-size bowl combine the flour, baking powder and salt; set aside. In another medium-size bowl, using an electric mixer, cream the margarine and sugar. Beat in the eggs, one at a time, then beat in the lemon peel and juice and the flavoring extract. Gradually add the dry ingredients, beating constantly for 1 to 2 minutes, or until almost incorporated. Add the currants and apricots, and beat for 1 minute more, or just until combined. Divide and shape the dough into two 2 1/2-inch-thick loaves. Place them on a nonstick baking sheet and bake for 30 minutes, or until just beginning to brown. Let the loaves cool on a rack for 45 minutes.

   Preheat the broiler. Place the loaves on a cutting board and, with a serrated knife, cut them diagonally into 3/8-inch-thick slices. Lay them on a baking sheet and broil 5 inches from the heat for 1 minute, or until lightly browned. Carefully turn the biscotti and brown them for another minute. Transfer them to a rack to cool, then store in an airtight container.   Makes 48 biscotti

APPLE-PUMPKIN CHEWIES

These soft cookies pack well, making them a good choice for a hike or picnic dessert. The pumpkin keeps them moist and is an excellent source of vitamin A, which plays a role in glycogen synthesis.

CALORIES per cookie	28
86% Carbohydrate	6 g
7% Protein	1 g
7% Fat	.2 g
CALCIUM	14 mg
IRON	.3 mg
SODIUM	18 mg

Vegetable cooking spray
2 large Granny Smith apples
1 cup canned pumpkin
1/4 cup molasses
1/4 cup brown sugar
1 teaspoon grated lemon peel
1/2 teaspoon vanilla extract

1 cup unbleached
  all-purpose flour
1/4 cup rolled oats
1 1/2 teaspoons baking powder
1/2 teaspoon ground ginger
Pinch of salt
1 egg, lightly beaten

Preheat the oven to 350° F. Spray a nonstick baking sheet with cooking spray; set aside. Wash and core but do not peel the apples. Grate the apples into a medium-size bowl; you should have about 2 cups. Add the pumpkin, molasses, sugar, lemon peel and vanilla and stir to combine; set aside. In a large bowl stir together the flour, oats, baking powder, ginger and salt, and make a well in the center. Add the egg mixture and stir just until combined. Drop the batter by tablespoons onto the baking sheet and bake for 35 minutes, or until the cookies are golden. Transfer the cookies to a rack to cool. Repeat with the remaining batter. If not serving the cookies immediately, store them in an airtight container. When fresh, they have a moist center; after a few days they will be chewier. Makes 48 cookies

MOLASSES COOKIES

White sugar is made of carbohydrates, but has no other nutritional value. Molasses, however, contains trace amounts of the minerals potassium, calcium and iron.

1/2 cup light molasses
1/3 cup margarine, cut into
  1-tablespoon pieces
2 cups unbleached
  all-purpose flour

1/4 cup brown sugar
1 tablespoon skim milk
1 teaspoon ground ginger
1/2 teaspoon baking powder

Heat the molasses in a medium-size saucepan over medium-low heat. When the molasses reaches the boiling point, stir in the margarine. When the margarine has melted, remove the pan from the heat and stir in the flour, sugar, milk, ginger and baking powder. Stir until the mixture forms a thick dough that pulls away from the sides of the pan. Place the dough on a 12 x12-inch sheet of foil and let it cool for a few minutes, then form it into a 1 1/2-inch-thick roll about 10 inches long. Wrap the dough in the foil and refrigerate it for at least 3 hours, or until firm.

Preheat the oven to 325° F. Unwrap the dough and, with a sharp knife, cut it into 1/4-inch-thick slices. (Dip the knife briefly into warm water between cuts if the dough sticks to it.) Place the cookies 3/4 inch apart on a nonstick baking sheet and bake for 10 to 15 minutes, or until just firm to the touch. Transfer the cookies to a rack to cool; if not serving immediately, store them in an airtight container. Makes 40 cookies

CALORIES per cookie	52
68% Carbohydrate	9 g
5% Protein	1 g
27% Fat	2 g
CALCIUM	13 mg
IRON	.4 mg
SODIUM	24 mg

PEAR CUPCAKES

These lowfat, high-fiber cupcakes are a healthy dessert alternative to a slice of frosted cake. Skim milk is an excellent dietary source of calcium, which is important in neuromuscular functioning and in the breakdown of glycogen in the muscles as well as in maintaining bone density and overall strength.

1 firm-ripe Comice pear	1/3 cup brown sugar
2 cups unbleached all-purpose flour	1 egg, lightly beaten
1/2 cup yellow cornmeal	1/2 teaspoon orange extract
2 teaspoons baking powder	1/2 teaspoon grated orange peel
2 tablespoons plus 1 teaspoon margarine	1 cup skim milk

Preheat the oven to 375° F. Line 12 muffin tin cups with paper liners; set aside. Wash and core but do not peel the pear. Grate the pear into a small bowl; you should have about 1 cup. In another small bowl combine the flour, cornmeal and baking powder; set aside. In a medium-size bowl cream together the margarine and sugar, then gradually beat in the egg, orange extract and orange peel. Stir in the pear, then add half the milk and half the dry ingredients, and stir to combine. Add the remaining milk and dry ingredients, and stir just until combined; do not overmix. Divide the batter among the muffin tin cups (they will be about 3/4 full) and bake for 30 to 35 minutes, or until the cupcakes are golden and a toothpick inserted in a cupcake comes out clean and dry. Transfer the cupcakes to a rack to cool before serving.

Makes 12 cupcakes

CALORIES per cupcake	156
78% Carbohydrate	30 g
10% Protein	4 g
12% Fat	2 g
CALCIUM	74 mg
IRON	1 mg
SODIUM	105 mg

APPLE FREEZE

Most fruit-based frozen desserts are higher in carbohydrates than ice cream, but some contain heavy cream and are high in fat. This smooth but nearly fat-free dessert is made with lowfat yogurt, and including the apple peels makes it high in pectin, an especially beneficial form of dietary fiber.

2 1/2 pounds apples, preferably a combination of Granny Smith and Red Delicious	2 tablespoons lemon juice
	1/2 cup plain lowfat yogurt
1/2 cup sugar	1 egg white
	1/4 teaspoon ground cinnamon

Wash and core but do not peel the apples, and cut them into large chunks. Place them in a food processor or blender and process for 1 to 2 minutes, or until puréed. Add the sugar and lemon juice, and process for another minute, or until well blended. Add the yogurt, egg white and cinnamon, and process for 1 minute more. Transfer the mixture to the container of an ice-cream maker and freeze it for 20 minutes, or according to the manufacturer's instructions, until firm.

If not serving the apple freeze immediately, cover the container tightly and place it in the freezer. If necessary, let it soften at room temperature for 5 minutes, or until soft enough to scoop, before serving. Divide the apple freeze among 4 dessert dishes, and serve.

Makes 8 servings

CALORIES per serving	137
92% Carbohydrate	34 g
4% Protein	1 g
4% Fat	1 g
CALCIUM	37 mg
IRON	3 mg
SODIUM	17 mg

Snacks and Beverages

CORN THINS

Unlike many packaged snacks, these crackers are low in sodium.

CALORIES per cracker	10
76% Carbohydrate	2 g
9% Protein	.2 g
15% Fat	.2 g
CALCIUM	2 mg
IRON	.1 mg
SODIUM	15 mg

1 cup white cornmeal,
  approximately
1/2 cup unbleached
  all-purpose flour
1 tablespoon sugar
1/2 teaspoon salt

1/4 teaspoon baking soda
1/4 teaspoon ground pepper,
  or more to taste
1/2 cup plain lowfat yogurt
1 tablespoon margarine, melted
Vegetable cooking spray

Preheat the oven to 350° F. In a medium-size bowl combine 1 cup of cornmeal, the flour, sugar, salt, baking soda and pepper. Add the yogurt and margarine and stir until combined. Divide the dough into 2 portions. Spray a nonstick baking sheet with cooking spray; lightly dust a rolling pin with cornmeal. Place one portion of dough on the baking sheet and roll it out to a 1/4-inch thickness. Place a sheet of plastic wrap over the dough and roll it out to a 10 x 10-inch square. Remove the plastic wrap. Using a ruler and a sharp knife, cut the dough into 2-inch squares, then into triangles; do not separate them. Bake the crackers for 20 minutes, or until crisp and golden. Check after 8 minutes; if the crackers are browning unevenly, turn the baking sheet. With a metal spatula, transfer the crackers to a rack to cool (they will separate as you remove them from the pan). Wash and respray the baking sheet, then make a second batch of corn thin crackers in the same fashion.   Makes 100 crackers

Corn Thins

ALMOST-CHOCOLATE MUFFINS

The rich flavor of pumpernickel bread, combined with vanilla, gives these muffins a chocolatelike taste. They freeze well and are good to have on hand for a quick carbohydrate boost before or after exercise. A packaged chocolate cupcake would have about twice the fat and one fourth the calcium.

CALORIES per muffin	142
74% Carbohydrate	27 g
12% Protein	4 g
14% Fat	2 g
CALCIUM	89 mg
IRON	1 mg
SODIUM	243 mg

3 cups fresh pumpernickel bread crumbs (about 6 slices of bread)
1 cup unbleached all-purpose flour
2 teaspoons baking powder
1/4 teaspoon salt

2 eggs
1/2 cup brown sugar
1 tablespoon margarine, melted
1 teaspoon vanilla extract
1 cup skim milk

Preheat the oven to 375° F. Line 12 muffin tin cups with paper liners; set aside. In a medium-size bowl combine the bread crumbs, flour, baking powder and salt; set aside. Beat the eggs in another medium-size bowl, then beat in the sugar, margarine and vanilla. Add half of the milk, then half of the dry ingredients and stir until combined. Add the remaining milk and dry ingredients and stir just until combined; do not overmix. Divide the batter among the muffin tin cups (they will be about 3/4 full) and bake for 25 minutes, or until the cupcakes are brown and a toothpick inserted in a cupcake comes out clean and dry. Transfer the muffins to a rack to cool before serving.

Makes 12 muffins

DOSAS

In India, the griddle breads called dosas are served plain or stuffed with a filling such as spiced potatoes. The Vegetable Purée on page 131 would make a good topping for these multi-grain breads. You could also use cottage cheese with a pinch of curry powder mixed in. For a sweet snack, you might spread the dosas with Chunky Fruit Butter (page 131) or crushed berries.

CALORIES per dosa	105
84% Carbohydrate	22 g
12% Protein	3 g
4% Fat	1 g
CALCIUM	30 mg
IRON	1 mg
SODIUM	103 mg

1 1/3 cups yellow cornmeal
1/3 cup whole-wheat flour
1/3 cup unbleached all-purpose flour

1/2 teaspoon salt
2/3 cup cooked brown rice
1 cup skim milk
Vegetable cooking spray

In a medium-size bowl combine the cornmeal, whole-wheat flour, all-purpose flour and salt. Add the rice, milk and 3/4 cup of water, and stir until the mixture forms a batter. Cover the bowl with plastic wrap and set aside at room temperature for 1 hour.

Spray a large nonstick skillet with cooking spray and heat it over medium-high heat. Pour in 4 scant 1/4-cup portions of batter and cook them for about 2 1/2 minutes, or until tiny holes form in the surface and the batter appears slightly dry. Turn the dosas and cook for another 2 minutes, or until the second side is dry. Serve the dosas hot or warm; they may also be eaten cold but they will not be as tender.

Makes 12 dosas

PROP CREDITS

Cover: swimsuit, goggles, tank top and running shorts–The Finals, Port Jervis, N.Y.; page 6: swimsuit–Hind Performance Sportswear, San Luis Obispo, Calif.; pages 24-31: T-shirt and stirrup pants–Athletic Style, New York City, mat–AMF American, Jefferson, Iowa; page 32: swimsuit–Hind Performance Sportswear, San Luis Obispo, Calif.; pages 36-57: swimsuit and cap–Hind Performance Sportswear, San Luis Obispo, Calif., goggles- The Finals, Port Jervis, N.Y.; page 47: flotation device–The Finals, Port Jervis, N.Y.; page 52: kickboard–The Finals, Port Jervis, N.Y.; pages 58-63: leotard and shorts–Athletic Style, New York City, sneakers–Nautilus Athletic Footwear, Inc., Greenville, S.C., dumbbells–Bollinger Industries, Inc., Irving, Texas, ankle weights–Excel: The Exercise Co., Pico Rivera, Calif.; page 64: helmet–Giro, Santa Cruz, Calif., gloves–Spenco, Waco, Texas, cycling shoes–Lake Sport, courtesy of Look America, Highland Park, Ill., cycling jersey–Hind Performance Sportswear, San Luis Obispo, Calif., cycling shorts–The Finals, Port Jervis, N.Y., bicycle–John Howard Signature Line by KHS, Carson, Calif.; page 68: bicycle–City Cycles, New York City; page 69: bicycle–Stuyvesant Bicycle Co., New York City; pages 70-71: cycling shoes–Nike, Inc., Beaverton, Ore., gloves, water bottle, helmets, saddle and cyclocomputer–Stuyvesant Bicycle Co., New York City; pages 72-89: gloves–Hind Performance Sportswear, San Luis Obispo, Calif., cycling shoes–Lake Sport, courtesy of Look America, Highland Park, Ill., helmet–Giro, Santa Cruz, Calif., cycling shorts–DaVinci, courtesy of The Alexis Corp., Miami, Fla., cycling jersey–The Finals, Port Jervis, N.Y., bicycle–John Howard Signature Line by KHS, Carson, Calif.; page 76: home trainer–Medalist, courtesy of Palo Alto Bicycles, Palo Alto, Calif.; pages 92-97: gloves–Hind Performance Sportswear, San Luis Obispo, Calif., cycling shoes–Lake Sport, courtesy of Look America, Highland Park, Ill., helmet–Giro, Santa Cruz, Calif., cycling shorts and jersey–The Finals, Port Jervis, N.Y., bicycle–John Howard Signature Line by KHS, Carson, Calif.; pages 98-103: tank top, shorts and sneakers–Athletic Style, New York City; page 111: cycling shorts and top–Dave Scott Signature Line by InSport, Beaverton, Ore., helmet and cycling shoes–Avenir, Newbury Park, Calif., bicycle–Dave Scott Ironman by Centurion, Newbury Park, Calif., handlebars–Profile For Speed, Inc., Chicago, Ill.; page 112: running clothes–Dave Scott Signature Line by InSport, Beaverton, Ore.; pages 114-117: swimsuit and goggles–Dave Scott Signature Line by InSport, Beaverton, Ore.; pages 118-119: cycling shorts and top–Dave Scott Signature Line by InSport, Beaverton, Ore., helmet and cycling shoes–Avenir, Newbury Park, Calif., bicycle–Dave Scott Ironman by Centurion, Newbury Park, Calif., handlebars–Profile For Speed, Inc., Chicago, Ill.; pages 120-121: running clothes–Dave Scott Signature Line by InSport, Beaverton, Ore.; pages 122-123: top and briefs–Dave Scott Signature Line by InSport, Beaverton, Ore., helmet and cycling shoes–Avenir, Newbury Park, Calif., bicycle–Dave Scott Ironman by Centurion, Newbury Park, Calif., handlebars–Profile For Speed, Inc., Chicago, Ill., sunglasses–Smith, Newbury Park, Calif.; page 128: salt and pepper shakers and napkin holder–Gear Stores, New York City; page 134: plates and linen–Ad Hoc Softwares, New York City, glasses–Thaxton & Co., New York City; page 137: linens–Ad Hoc Softwares, New York City; page 140: bowl–Thaxton & Co., New York City, glass–Sointu, New York City.

ACKNOWLEDGMENTS

All cosmetics and grooming products supplied by Clinique Labs, Inc., New York City

Nutrition analysis provided by Hill Nutrition Associates, Fayetteville, N.Y.

Off-camera warm-up equipment: rowing machine supplied by Precor USA, Redmond, Wash.; Tunturi stationary bicycle supplied by Amerec Corp., Bellevue, Wash.

Washing machine and dryer supplied by White-Westinghouse, Columbus, Ohio

Index prepared by Ian Tucker

Production by Giga Communications

PHOTOGRAPHY CREDITS

Indoor exercise photography and photograph on page 6: Andrew Eccles; outdoor photography: ©David Madison 1988; photographs on pages 90, 91, 104, 105: ©David Epperson/ WILDPIC.

ILLUSTRATION CREDITS

Pages 8, 9, 10, illustrations: David Flaherty; page 14, chart, illustration: Phil Scheuer; pages 19, 20, 21, 23, charts: Brian Sisco; pages 78, 90, 91, illustrations: Phil Scheuer; pages 108, 109, 110, 113, charts: Brian Sisco.

Index